Ballooning

Ballooning

From basics to record breaking

John Christopher

The Crowood Press

First published in 2001 by
The Crowood Press Ltd
Ramsbury, Marlborough
Wiltshire SN8 2HR

British Library Cataloguing-in-Publication Data
A catalogue record for this book is available from the British Library.

ISBN 1 86126 423 2

Line drawings by David Fisher.

Typeset by Phoenix Typesetting, Ilkley, West Yorkshire

Printed and bound in Great Britain by Antony Rowe, Chippenham

Contents

Foreword 7

Acknowledgements 8

Introduction 9

1 Getting Started 13

2 Requirements for a Licence 17

3 The Hot-Air Balloon 21

4 Equipment 36

5 Preflight Preparation 42

6 Getting off the Ground 49

7 In Flight 60

8 The Art of Retrieving 71

9 Propane – Fuel to Fly 78

10 Putting on a Show 85

11 Advanced Ballooning 91

12 Ground School 102

Glossary of Abbreviations 122

Conversion Factors 123

Further Information 124

Index 126

Foreword

I have spent more than twenty years climbing the highest peaks around the world and man-hauling sledges or sailing boats to the poles, but I have never experienced anything like the extraordinary events that took place on my miracle balloon flight to within eight miles of the North Pole in May 2000.

I had taken up ballooning just three years earlier. It was while trudging in –90°C windchill towards the North Pole that I decided that it would be an easier alternative for an 'adventure rush' – everybody makes some mistakes. As a novice pilot with only five hours on my licence I had tackled the Andes Mountains crossing with the *Typhoo Challenger*, succeeding on the second attempt after a hairy three and a half hour roller-coaster ride.

But for me the polar flight, emulating the courageous but ill-fated gas balloon expedition of Salomon Andrée over a century earlier, was the real reason I had taken up ballooning. I cannot describe the fear I felt or the beauty I experienced as I took off in the *Britannic Challenger* balloon, out of a valley and across the peaks of Spitsbergen. I was sitting on my makeshift seat, a cool box, thinking how extraordinarily lucky I was to be doing this. Little did I realize that after a flight of five and a half days the capricious winds would carry me back to Spitsbergen for a thirty-minute drag-landing through freezing water, over ice and into ice boulders.

Yes, we broke records, but for me what this flight showed was that like-minded people with a simple belief in something can do anything. In ballooning not only had I discovered a whole new world of adventure and challenge, but also I found myself in a community of enthusiasts who went out of their way to make me welcome.

When I was training for my licence an up-to-date and comprehensive guide to ballooning was hard to find, so I welcome this new manual by John Christopher who has done so much to promote the sport over the years. Written by a pilot, this manual has it all and it is with the added advantage of including relevant information and not simply waffle. A great read for the amateur or the professional alike.

Whatever your involvement, ballooning makes the world all the more exciting. My only regret is I didn't start twenty years ago.

David Hempleman-Adams

David Hempleman-Adams during training for his balloon flight to the North Pole in 2000.

Acknowledgements

I am grateful to the BBAC for their co-operation in the production of this book and for permission to reproduce the Code of Conduct and other information. In particular I must thank the BBAC Training Officer Rick Hatton for his assistance, and the other officers of the club who either provided information or assisted by checking the typescript. Acknowledgement must also be paid to the previous BBAC Training Officers, Mike Moore and Brian Jones, who have worked so hard in establishing the club's good training practices over the years.

For additional assistance I would like to thank: Ian Ashpole, David Bareford, Don Cameron, Martin Casson, Graeme Clark, Chris Lynch, Wyn Morgan, Tony Pinner and Peter Vale. Special thanks go to David Hempleman-Adams for contributing the foreword and for keeping the spirit of ballooning adventure alive, and to Ute for all her hard work and encouragement.

The following individuals and organizations have generously supplied the photographs for this book: Michael Ball, David and Karin Bareford, Rob Bayly, Peter Blazer, Breitling, Chas Breton, Britannic Assurance, Rod Buck, Cameron Balloons, Ian Culley and the Dante Group, Peter Dowlen of J. Bennett & Son, Phil Dunnington, Mandy Dickinson, John Eveson of the *Farmer's Guardian*, Ute Feierabend, Flying Pictures, Bob Garnett, John Gray, Pete Johnson, Lindstrand Balloons, Olli Luoma and the Light in the Night Group, Robin Macey, Ed Macholc, Neil McCulloch, Chris Nicholson, Graeme Pusey, Sky Balloons, Mark Stevens, Bill Teasdale, Thunder & Colt, Bob Trotter, David Usill of Window on the World, Virgin Airship & Balloon Company, and Tony Wiseman Photography.

All additional photography by John Christopher.

Introduction

Hot-air ballooning is an air sport that can be enjoyed by anyone; it offers so many different things to different people. For some the greatest pleasure is to be found floating in an overgrown laundry basket with a gentle breeze, thousands of feet above a countryside that is lent fresh hues with each passing season – a timeless experience in which familiar hills, woods and towns take on a whole new perspective and the cares of the world are left far below. But for others it is a matter of pushing themselves and their machines to the limit, experiencing that exhilarating adrenalin rush of ballooning right at the edge, competing with one another in national or international championships, taking on the challenge of setting new records or flying in places where no one has gone before.

When the *Breitling Orbiter 3* touched down on a remote Egyptian plateau at the end of its successful twenty-day non-stop circumnavigation of the world in March 1999, it seemed to many in the sport that ballooning had reached its zenith. It was a fantastic achievement but we had, they suggested, climbed our 'Everest' and there was nowhere else to go. But they were wrong. Ballooning continues to evolve and there are still many new adventures to be had on all levels. It remains an exciting and rewarding activity, a great way to see the world and to explore your own skills.

A Brief History

Ballooning is the earliest and perhaps the purest form of flying. Its origins go back more

The powerful burners that give modern hot-air balloons their lift.

9

In September 1783 the Montgolfier brothers sent up a sheep, a duck and a cockerel two months before the first manned flight.

Parisian scientific establishment backed its own alternative line of development led by Professor Charles, and just ten days after the Montgolfier's first demonstration of manned flight his hydrogen-filled balloon took to the skies. The problem for the proponents of the hot-air variety was that their craft were bigger than the gas balloons, for hot-air is much less efficient as a lifting medium, and they were inherently more fragile and prone to mishap, carrying aloft with them their own means of fiery self-destruction. The rest, as they say is history, and it was the gas balloon that came to dominate the lighter-than-air scene for almost two centuries.

Then, in the late 1950s, the hot-air balloon experienced a remarkable resurgence of interest from a most unlikely source. Under the auspices of the US Navy it was being evaluated as a means of rescuing downed fighter pilots and, more covertly, as a method of placing American agents behind enemy lines. The result of this research brought together the two essential elements of the modern hot-air balloon – man-made fabrics for a lightweight and airtight envelope, with propane gas as an efficient and safe source of generating the necessary heat. Giving this new lease on life the sport of hot-air ballooning has flourished to such an extent that it is the gas balloon that is now the rarer of the two.

BALLOONING TODAY

Huge strides have been made in balloon technology in the last few decades, especially with the introduction of computer-aided design and manufacturing techniques, and the development of the modern burners, which are incredibly powerful and to some extent getting quieter with each new generation. The result is a safe and reliable craft that is great fun to fly, and consequently

than two hundred years to 1783 when the Montgolfier brothers, paper manufacturers from the little town of Annonay in southern France, captured the lifting properties of what they mistakenly called 'phlogiston', for they believed that it was the smoke itself that held the key – although their flimsy craft constructed of paper and cotton were in fact carried aloft by the heat from burning faggots of straw. Not to be outdone, the

Balloons jostle for space within the congested arena of the Bristol International Balloon Fiesta.

numbers have increased dramatically. On a calm summer's evening the bright colours of hot-air balloons have become a regular feature of the landscape in many parts of the world – balloonists are particularly active in the UK (where it is estimated that there are around 600 pilots), the USA, Germany, France and other parts of Europe, in Australia, Canada and in Japan.

In addition, the balloon gatherings or 'meets', once the province of small bands of private balloonists, have in many cases expanded into large international events. Commercialism has had an impact too with an ever-increasing number of advertising balloons (often in weird and wonderful shapes) promoting their clients' wares or services, plus the emergence of the passenger-rides business in some countries. Arguably this means that ballooning has become more widely accessible – which in itself can be no bad thing – and given a year of reasonably good weather in the UK tens of thousands of people will get their first taste of the high life. And the good news is that ballooning remains one of the safest forms of recreational flying with an enviable record for safety.

ABOUT THIS BOOK

This book has been written with two main objectives: to serve as a useful and informative introduction to the sport of hot-air ballooning, and to provide the basic answers to anyone wishing to get more directly involved. It explains how to get some hands-on experience before you jump in; the practicalities of buying and operating a balloon; the requirements for obtaining a pilot's licence, both practical and ground school; the balloon systems themselves from the theory of how a balloon flies to its component parts and their construction; the other essential equipment needed to get the job done; and the whole process of flying from the pre-flight preparations including passenger and crew briefings, through control in flight, fuel management and the landing. Emergency procedures and handling propane are also examined.

Once you have obtained that precious licence you may want to take matters further by attending balloon events or by putting on displays. If that's not enough there is a section on competitive flying, setting new records, night flying and the sort of extreme ballooning your grandmother should have warned you about!

While every effort has been made to produce an authoritative introduction to ballooning, there are often differing opinions about exactly how to go about certain things. I have attempted to produce a consensus of these, largely guided by the UK system devised by the British Balloon & Airship Club. Different countries have their own variations on these training requirements and in addition, despite attempts to harmonize international aviation regulations, there are still large areas of air law that vary from country to country. Accordingly the contact addresses for the appropriate national organizations are included in Further Information to point you in the right direction. It is also beyond the scope of any single volume to provide all the information necessary to pass the written examinations, so a list of recommended further reading is included.

But do bear in mind that you don't have to become a pilot in order to enjoy ballooning and countless retrieve crew members play a vital and often unsung role in every successful flight. Which is why a whole section is devoted to the art of retrieving and the role of both pilot *and* crew as aerial ambassadors for our sport.

Whatever your area of involvement, I hope this book will serve to whet your appetite and to provide the foundation for some safe and enjoyable flying.

1 Getting Started

TRY IT FIRST

'How long does it take to learn to fly a balloon?'

This is just about the most frequently asked question any balloon pilot is likely to hear. 'How long is a piece of string?' might be the glib answer. So let's begin with the good news – flying a balloon is not that difficult. Balloon-builder Don Cameron likens it to driving a car. 'Anyone who can drive a car can learn to fly a modern hot-air balloon. It is an uncomplicated craft and its control in fair weather can be adequately mastered by any normal person.' But, and it's an important 'but', the key to flying a balloon well is experience, experience and more experience.

And 'experience' is a word that crops up again for the newcomer – before you start

down this path make sure that ballooning really is for you. That may sound blindingly obvious, but sometimes people are beguiled by the image and they buy a brand new balloon only to discover later on that they don't really like the way of life that goes with it; getting up before sunrise at the height of the summer for a start. Ballooning can easily become an all-consuming activity. It requires a good deal of time and effort on your part and accordingly it should also be your passion, and hopefully one that your partner or family will want to share.

So if you have never been in a balloon, try it first. Perhaps the easiest way to do this is to book a pleasure flight with one of the balloon operating companies and your telephone directory should list the nearest. I know of many cases where a single flight has

Hot-air balloons never fail to attract attention.

The camaraderie of a balloon syndicate; here the Dante Group celebrates another successful flight.

led from one thing to another until the victim has become a fully signed-up balloon owner and pilot. Alternatively, go and find some local balloonists: get in touch with your national balloon club – in the UK this is the British Balloon & Airship Club (BBAC), which also has regional groups covering most of the country. Offer your services as voluntary crew and in that way you are more likely get a realistic idea of what the ballooning scene is all about before you part with too much of your hard-earned cash. Most private pilots could use an extra pair of helping hands and in return they will usually offer the occasional flight to their crew. You may even find that this type of involvement is in itself a satisfying pastime.

BUYING A BALLOON

'How much does a balloon cost?' must rank as the most frequently asked question No.2.

Without reference to my piece of string I usually ask the questioner to guess what the balloon they are riding in would cost to replace and, almost without exception, they pitch in at about one third of the actual cost. Balloons are not cheap and this is because they are literally individually built by hand to the exacting standards you expect of any flying machine in which you will entrust your life.

So what will it all cost? This depends on what you want from your balloon, and once again the car provides a good analogy. The most basic balloon kit, say to carry two to three people, will cost roughly the same as a medium-sized car. But if you want an all-singing all-dancing model you'd be looking at a pretty high-spec executive car. And as with cars there is also a healthy second-hand market that often provides an opening for beginners to the sport. But to avoid ending up with a 'lemon' – or in ballooning parlance a balloon that is so porous it is referred to as a 'net' – do get someone with

A hot-air balloon packs away into a surprisingly compact trailer for transportation and storage between flights.

some experience to advise you before you buy.

For new balloons don't forget to shop around a little. There are several excellent balloon manufacturers and most are more than happy to discuss your requirements, offer advice and supply information on their products. Given a little advance notice they will often give guided tours of their factories so that you see for yourself how a balloon is constructed, and many also host special open days for existing and potential customers. Some addresses are given in Further Information, at the end of this book, and the Internet is an excellent way to go global window-shopping.

Of course there are ways to help keep the costs more manageable and sponsorship, in the form of advertising on the envelope, is one way that many balloonists have adopted. But this route is not really for the beginner as there is seldom something for nothing and most sponsors will have certain expectations

in return for their largesse. In addition, regardless of your ability to deliver results, you could fall foul of the rules regarding 'aerial work' – more on that later.

You might do better forming a syndicate – although this is not a term favoured in the USA where it has connotations with the Mob! Call it what you will, a syndicate is an effective means of sharing the costs and it comes with the added bonus of providing a group of like-minded individuals who, in theory, will be there to help each other. Joining a typical syndicate of four or maybe five people has obvious advantages in getting the money together to buy a new or second-hand balloon, perhaps a smaller model that will be easy to operate and handle on the ground. Such a system can work very well and it is quite common in gliding circles for example. However, joining a balloon syndicate has been compared to getting married and you must be sure that you will be able to get along with the other people (and their families). If you are going to co-exist happily, a firm foundation for any new syndicate involves clearly defining the ground rules concerning the financial commitment (initial input as well as running costs), such matters as who gets to use the balloon when and where, who has priority in training and the mechanism for selling-on a share. But be warned: there are several documented cases where ballooning has been cited in the divorce courts and, as with marriage, while many syndicates result in life-long friendships others end up in acrimonious argument.

OPERATING COSTS

The third question I am most often asked is how much does it cost to run a balloon. And by that most people mean the cost of the propane fuel. Yes this is a factor, but you may be surprised to learn that it is a relatively minor one as there are several other expenses to be considered.

Firstly there is the depreciation in the value of the balloon itself. Mostly because of ultraviolet degradation, the average balloon envelope can optimistically be expected to last for around only 400 flights or so before it becomes too porous. Maybe even fewer if it has been badly abused or frequently over-loaded. So a sobering exercise is to divide the cost of your envelope by that number of expected flights and get an approximate depreciation figure per flight. The other equipment such as the basket, burners and fuel cylinders is much more hardwearing than the envelope.

Then there is the transportation of the balloon. If you opt for a trailer then you are going to need a vehicle capable of pulling it – sometimes in and out of muddy fields – and most family cars are simply not up to the job. As an alternative to an expensive 4×4 and trailer some balloonists prefer a self-contained van, but either way, running your retrieve vehicle can be almost as expensive as running the balloon.

Then there are the 'paper' costs: insurance cover for the balloon, including third party in case you cause damage to other people's property or animals, plus insurance for the other equipment against damage or theft. Your balloon will need to be inspected annually to ensure that it is airworthy. Although such inspections are not mandatory with privately owned balloons in the UK at the time of writing, most balloonists choose to have them done for their own peace of mind and also because some event organizers insist upon it.

Don't forget wear and tear on the equipment, the odd repair, maps, radios, plus regular medicals for the pilots, subscriptions to the national balloon organization, obtaining weather information and so on and so on. I know the list sounds endless; nonetheless ballooning remains one of the cheapest forms of recreational flying. It attracts people from all walks of life and, at the end of the day, it is terrific fun.

But what about training? More good news – depending on how you go about it, training to become a balloon pilot need not be that expensive . . . read on.

2 Requirements for a Licence

MINIMUM REQUIREMENTS FOR PPL(B)

Despite some movement towards harmonization, the requirements for a balloon pilot's licence still vary considerably between different countries. In the UK all licences are issued by the Civil Aviation Authority (CAA) and they publish the full legal requirements in a section of the Civil Aviation Publication 53 (CAP 53) – details of where to obtain copies of this and other publications are given in Further Information. Almost without exception, training and examination for the Private Pilot's Licence (Balloons) or PPL(B) is taken care of by the British Balloon & Airship Club, the governing body of the sport of ballooning in the UK, through its own system of approved instructors and CAA-approved examiners. This ensures that any candidate – a 'PuT' or 'Pilot under Training' – meets the requirements of the CAA, and some additional ones imposed by the BBAC itself, and all of these are listed here:

- A minimum flying experience of sixteen hours (undertaken within a twelve-month period).
- A minimum of six flights of which at least four have to be taken with a BBAC approved Instructor – the rest may be with any valid PPL(B).
- To keep a flight log book with flight training records completed by the instructing pilot. (The BBAC also requires all candidates to keep a PuT Training Log Book.)
- Once recommended by a BBAC approved Instructor, to undertake a Flight Test with a CAA-approved Examiner.
- Perform a solo flight under the supervision of the Examiner or an Instructor delegated by the Examiner.

Anyone can learn to fly a hot-air balloon.

- To pass written examinations in Aviation Law, Navigation, Meteorology, Airmanship and Balloon Systems, and Human Performance & Limitations.
- Obtain countersignature of self-declaration of fitness by your doctor.
- The BBAC also requires all pilots to attend an approved Landowner Relations course.
- To be issued with a PPL(B) a candidate must be seventeen years old. However, the CAA permits training and testing to be conducted from the age of sixteen.

By comparison the requirements for the PPL in the USA seem a little less demanding, with a minimum of ten hours of flight training conducted by a CPL qualified pilot, plus a check-out and solo flight signed off by a Designated Flight Instructor (DFI). In addition there are only three written examinations set by the Federal Aviation Authority (FAA).

Time Constraints

It is very important to point out that the UK requirements have a limited life span, usually twelve months, so some care must be taken in studying the rules to ensure that you complete the necessary qualifications within a valid time scale. There's nothing worse than building up your hours only to discover that your exam passes have expired in the meantime, or vice versa.

PRACTICAL FLIGHT TRAINING

Unlike fixed-wing flying, or gliding for that matter, ballooning is a 'green field' air sport with no clubhouses and virtually no club balloons. Therefore the first question that any prospective balloon pilot must ask himself or herself is whether they have access to a balloon. It's the prime factor that directly affects the cost of training because using someone else's balloon and equipment can prove to be very expensive. If you have a balloon, or a share in one, then obtaining training becomes much more straightforward as, for the most part, it can be conducted by any qualified balloon pilot and many will gladly fly with you at your expense. You will, however, still need the minimum number of instructor flights and an examiner flight for which you will most likely be charged.

Perhaps the minimum requirement of sixteen hours does not seem that onerous, but keep in mind that this is only a minimum and most PuTs require twenty or so hours before they feel ready to check out, sometimes even more, and in the UK this could easily take the best part of a year to achieve.

So how do you clock-up these hours? There are various approaches and, although it may all appear to be about money, it has in fact more to do with common sense. One option, if you can afford it, is to go to one of the flying schools overseas where you know that good flying weather is almost guaranteed – even use their balloons and crew if you don't have your own – fly with them every available slot and so accumulate your hours in maybe a couple of weeks. Alternatively, you can train in the UK, getting to grips with the ever-changing flying conditions served up by the vagaries of the weather. This is sure to take longer, and certainly there is nothing more frustrating than waiting for the weather to improve when you are itching to get on, but the general consensus is that this approach will give the new pilot a much broader base of experience on which to build.

Of course there are many instructors situated within the UK to take you through your training and, in addition, many of the balloon manufacturers offer their own training facilities or have links with particular flying schools. Information is available from the national ballooning clubs and if you do go down this route you will discover that costs vary, so do shop around.

In either event there will be fees for sitting the examinations – a great incentive to make sure you pass perhaps – for the check-out flight with an Examiner, and in addition the CAA will charge quite a hefty fee to issue your new licence. Unfortunately these costs all tend to change with monotonous regularity.

EXAMS

Of the five written papers for the PPL(B), each has a pass mark of 70 per cent and negative marking is not employed where multiple choice questions are answered incorrectly. These papers may be taken by private arrangement with a BBAC examiner, through the manufacturers or at the CAA building at Gatwick.

It is a requirement of the BBAC that all written papers are passed prior to check-out, and it is mandatory that the Air Law examination has been passed prior to any solo flight. (*See* Chapter 12 for more on these exams.)

HEALTH RESTRICTIONS

In theory flying a hot-air balloon does not require any particular physical strength, and for the PPL the health restrictions are for the most part very tolerant. A person with only one eye, or someone with an artificial limb for example, will not be automatically exempted as long as they pass their medical and can demonstrate that they are up to the task on their check-out flight. However, there are some medical conditions that, at present at least, automatically bar a person from undertaking solo flights – in particular certain heart conditions, plus epilepsy and diabetes where the possibility of blackouts is considered to be too great a risk. Having said that, this shouldn't prevent someone from

*If it holds enough hot air it can fly –
a special-shape advertising balloon.*

learning how to fly a balloon without actually holding a licence as long as they are always accompanied by a qualified pilot.

Medicals

Once again the requirements vary from country to country. In the UK it is still possible for a PuT or PPL(B) to obtain a self-certification declaration of fitness to be signed by their own doctor, although some doctors may expect to undertake some sort of examination in order to do this. These certificates are valid for a five-year period for applicants up to thirty-nine years of age, two years for forty to forty-nine year olds, and for only twelve months for those who are fifty or over.

19

The requirements for the Commercial Pilots Licence CPL(B) medicals are more demanding and pilots are required to undergo examination by a CAA Authorized Medical Examiner (AME). As this is one area where international harmonization might produce changes in the next few years, you are advised to check with your national ballooning club or aviation authority for the most up-to-date requirements.

OTHER LICENCES

I well remember my solo check-out flight. Flying the balloon so lightly laden for the first time I shot up like a homesick angel, half exhilarated by the sense of freedom and the fact that there was no one looking over my shoulder, and half terrified by the knowledge that I was the only one in charge. Nevertheless, it took a long time to wipe the grin off my face, and the day that your coveted licence plops through the letter box is one you will never forget. But it is often said in ballooning circles that the PPL(B) is only a licence to *start* learning. And there is a degree of truth in this, for every flight brings new situations and new experiences that slowly build with time. Some wit once summed it up nicely, 'You start with a bagful of luck, and an empty bag of experience – the trick is to fill the latter before you run out of the former.'

For some pilots the PPL(B) will be enough for their level of participation in ballooning, but for the more career minded in the UK there are two types of CPL(B) licence: the 'Restricted' and the 'Full' or 'Unrestricted'. Basically a PPL can fly a sponsored balloon with everything paid for, but as soon as a sponsor asks you to attend an event it then becomes 'aerial work' and a CPL(B) is needed.

Both types of CPL(B) come with their own particular requirements. The CPL(B) Restricted, for example, includes thirty-five hours of flight time of which at least twenty must have been as P1 (the pilot in charge), two tethered flights, a flight test with a CAA-approved examiner and further written examinations. Until recently a UK Class 3 Medical Certificate was satisfactory, but as this no longer exists the CAA will probably accept a UK Class 2 or JAA Class 2 (the UK Class 2 is less onerous). The CAA is looking into the situation and you are advised to contact them before your medical test. The rules for the Full CPL(B) are even more rigorous, as this enables the holder to fly paying passengers, and they include seventy-five hours flying experience (which must include the minimum indicated for the Restricted Licence in addition to not less than sixty hours as P1), another flight test and a UK Class 2 medical.

For the PPL, once you have your licence further annual Flight Tests are not necessary, but for both forms of the CPL(B) they will be required. With all balloon pilot licences there are minimum annual flying hour requirements (five hours in the case of the PPL) and for the CPL(B) there is also the question of 'recency' which requires the pilot to have flown at least once in the preceding three months. Furthermore, the CAA has introduced size restrictions on the CPL(B) licences and the size of balloon that a commercial pilot can fly is dictated by the size he or she flew on the Flight Test.

3　The Hot-Air Balloon

THEORY OF BALLOONING

One of the great paradoxes of ballooning is that something so big in volume is actually lighter-than-air. And although the balloon's envelope is massive, when I am flying I find I become so absorbed by the gradually shifting panorama below and by the activity within the basket, that I often forget that the envelope is still there above our heads. It is like riding Aladdin's magic carpet and it usually takes some small noise, the tinkling of the burner coils cooling perhaps, to draw my eye upwards and into that nylon-wrapped bubble of hot air. Invisible to the eye, incredibly this is all that keeps us airborne, and as I add up the weight of the balloon itself, including the basket, the four heavy propane-filled cylinders plus several passengers, I can only marvel at this miracle of physics.

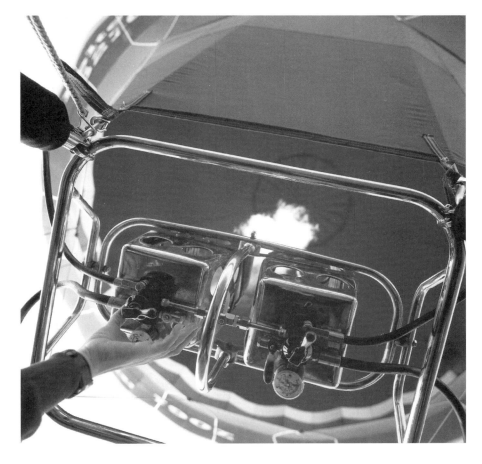

Applying the heat.

Traditional and modern helium-filled gas balloons line up at the start of a race from Alberquerque, New Mexico.

Every schoolchild knows that hot air rises and the reason is quite simple. If you take a given volume of air and warm it up it will expand, causing the number of molecules it contains to become less dense; hence it is lighter than the air at normal temperature. While 'ordinary' air may seem to be light it actually has a weight of just over 70lb per 1,000 cubic feet (cu ft) – the volume of a cube measuring 10ft along each side. By comparison, the heated air within a balloon's envelope weighs only 53lb per 1,000cu ft, and it is this 17lb difference between the two that can be described as the 'lift'. This figure will vary depending on the difference between the ambient air temperature and the internal temperature of the envelope, as well as the atmospheric pressure and the balloon's altitude.

Hot-air balloons have to be much bigger than gas balloons because hot air is less effective as a lifting medium. Hydrogen, the lightest gas of all, provides 65lb of lift per 1,000cu ft, a little over three times more than hot air, while its inert cousin helium offers 60lb. But filling a gas balloon with helium, only to vent it to the atmosphere at the end of the flight, is a very expensive form of ballooning by comparison with hot air and, despite the dramatically greater lift of a gas balloon, the popularity of hot air has more to do with its convenience and the considerably lower operating costs.

THE MODERN HOT-AIR BALLOON

The hot-air balloon is a gloriously simple flying machine and the advances made in recent years have resulted in one that is both reliable and very forgiving. Accidents are extremely rare and when they do occur it is almost always as the result of human error and not because of an equipment failure.

The illustration on the next page shows the basic anatomy of the hot-air balloon. From the top to the bottom: the envelope, which contains the hot air, is constructed of nylon or polyester fabrics reinforced with strong 'load tapes'. At the top of the envelope is the 'crown' where an opening, in this case the 'parachute' valve, provides an effective means of quickly spilling all that hot air upon landing. The vertical sections of the envelope are known as 'gores' and these are made up of several smaller panels. At the base or 'mouth', panels of fire-resistant Nomex protect the envelope from accidental heat damage. Steel 'flying wires' pass down from attachments at the bottom of the vertical load tapes to the burner or 'load frame' where they are connected by 'karabiners' to the frame and to the 'basket wires' which pass down through the wicker basket and up the other side to form a secure cradle. The burner or burners are situated in a gimballing frame within the burner frame so that they can be pointed in any direction during the inflation. The propane fuel is carried within 'flight cylinders' strapped inside the basket, and steel-lined hoses take the fuel from them to the burners.

There are many first-class balloon builders around the world and while basic details of their products may vary they all follow this basic layout. Some might offer triangular baskets or their own alternatives to the deflation systems, but at the end of the day it is all a matter of personal choice. As with a car it depends on whether you prefer the look and feel of a Ford compared with that say of a Volkswagen.

Balloon Sizes

When asked how tall their balloon is most pilots only have a vague idea. This is because balloon sizes are measured by the volume or capacity of the envelope and not by its height or circumference. In those countries that still adhere to some Imperial measurements, such as the UK and the USA, this is calculated in thousands of cubic feet, represented as '77,000cu ft' for example. In other countries balloonists and manufacturers prefer to work in cubic metres (cu m) and sadly there is no easy rule-of-thumb to convert between the two – conversion factors can be found at the end of this book. Often the size is abbreviated within the manufacturer's own designations, for example an LBL 105A (Lindstrand is the manufacturer, 105,000cu ft the volume and the 'A' indicating the number of gores) or a Cameron V65 (in this case built by Camerons, a 65,000cu ft 'Viva' model which has eight gores).

In ballooning, size really does matter! It is very important to get the right size for the job and this depends on many factors. How many people you need to lift, what the climate is like where you intend flying most often, and the number of crew available to handle the balloon and gear. In the first instance the number of people (pilot and/or passengers) can range from just one with the Cloudhopper-style seat and harness balloon of around 21,000cu ft or so, to the bigger 'people-movers' of 210,000cu ft for ten passengers and upwards. Most 'sport' balloonists opt for something around 77,000cu ft, as this will enable them to fly three to four people in most conditions and is small enough to easily handle on the ground and to transport. But as a general trend balloon sizes have been creeping up gradually and increasingly people now look to a 90,000cu ft balloon to do the same job.

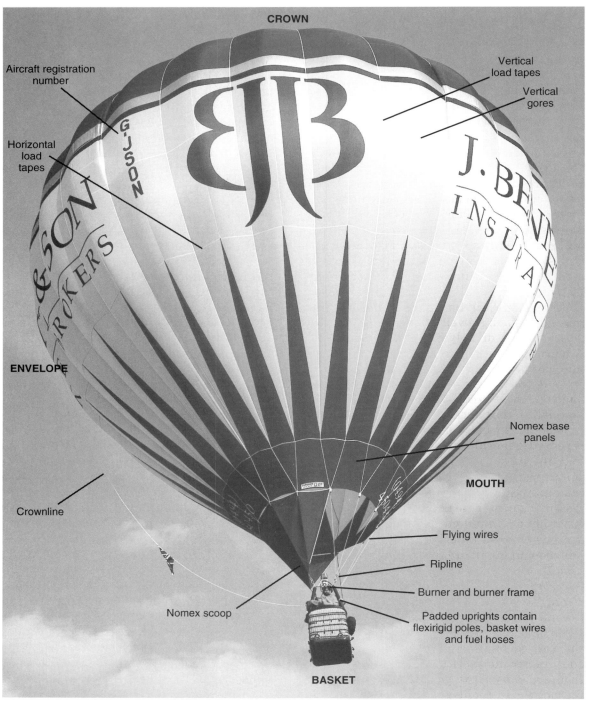

CROWN

Aircraft registration number

Vertical load tapes

Vertical gores

G-JSON

Horizontal load tapes

J. BEN

INSURA

& SON

ROKERS

ENVELOPE

Nomex base panels

MOUTH

Crownline

Flying wires

Ripline

Burner and burner frame

Nomex scoop

Padded uprights contain flexirigid poles, basket wires and fuel hoses

BASKET

The anatomy of a hot-air balloon.

Remember that it is the difference between internal and external temperature that makes a balloon fly and consequently when flying in hotter countries the amount of available lift is reduced. Atmospheric pressure also has a similar effect and for mountain flying it is better to err on the side of caution with a bigger envelope.

Envelopes

The overall inverted teardrop shape is a direct product of the envelope's function and results from mathematical formula designed for zero horizontal fabric stress. Fortunately the result is very pleasing to the eye and while one manufacturer may claim that their dome-topped envelope is more efficient than their competitor's flatter top there is little in it.

Modern hot-air balloon envelopes are constructed of lightweight man-made fibres, mostly nylon or polyester, coated with a polyurethane varnish to seal the gaps in the woven fabric. The main causes of balloon fabric degradation are ultraviolet light which is present in daylight, heat – especially if the balloon is over-heated, which is sometimes caused by over-loading – and repeated general handling. The result is that the envelope will eventually become porous to the point that an increase in fuel consumption will become apparent. The reassuring news here is that balloon fabric is generally one hundred times stronger than it needs to be in order to sustain the loads imposed upon it, and any deterioration should not compromise safety. It is likely that even minor damage will become evident during handling long before it poses a risk to the safety of the balloon in flight.

Balloon fabrics have greatly improved over the years and many manufacturers now offer longer-life fabrics for the top third of their balloons – the part that is obviously the hottest in flight as hot air rises – and although these fabrics tend to be slightly

A seamstress joins two panels with a load tape.

heavier and more expensive they can extend a balloon's performance considerably.

A balloon envelope is constructed from panels of fabric arranged in tapering, vertical sections known as 'gores' and the number of these will dictate the bulbousness of the balloon's appearance. An envelope with very few gores is the most bulbous, while a balloon with twenty-four or more gores is to all extents and purposes smooth sided. The bulbous gore is the most efficient as the curvature leads to low skin-tension, and the cheapest because of the amount of fabric used and the lower number of panels to be stitched. The smoother gore envelopes tend to be favoured by commercial companies who want a flatter surface on which to display their client's name or product.

The joins between the panels of fabric are usually made with what is known as a 'French felled seam' where the edge of each

A bulbous eight-gore Viva beside a smoother twenty-four-gore balloon.

panel is folded back on itself to interlock with the next, and then all four layers are stitched together. Various stitches are used in envelope construction and one of the main types is the lock stitch.

The main load-bearing strength of a hot-air balloon envelope comes not from the fabric itself but from strong load tapes situated on the vertical joins between the gores. Even though a bulbous balloon might have only eight, these are extremely strong with a one-inch (25mm) tubular nylon tape having a typical breaking strength of 4,000lb (1,800kg). A number of horizontal tapes are also incorporated into the envelope and they play a vital role in preventing rips from spreading, although they are not load bearing in flight.

At the base of the envelope, the part that is nearest to the burner, a ring of burn-resistant Nomex fabric reduces the risk of flame damage during inflation and protects the vertical load tapes. Because Nomex is resistant to coloured dyes a small amount of cotton is included in the weave and in instances where the flames have got a little too near this tends to burn off first leaving an unsightly but harmless scorched appearance. The Nomex itself is not completely burn-proof and a persistent pilot will eventually managed to scorch it to the point where it blackens and becomes friable. Burn damage to the bottom panels of the envelope caused during inflation used to be quite common, but nowadays the flames tend to be less feathery and the risk

The lighter area with the dark centre is the circular parachute valve in place at the top of an envelope.

is much reduced although not entirely eliminated.

Stainless steel wires lead down from the load tapes at the bottom of the envelope and are attached by karabiners to the load frame within which the burner sits. In order to prevent the flame being deflected across the open mouth – especially during inflation – it is almost universal to have an additional Nomex panel that extends from the bottom

Burners from two manufacturers showing the difference of styles and positioning of the burner controls.

of the envelope down to burner height. These come in two alternatives, the 'skirt', which is a cylinder held open by a strip of springed steel around its base, or the 'scoop', which fits across one side and attaches to two corners of the burner frame. During inflation the scoop ensures that any breeze is pushed up inside the envelope to improve internal pressurization and this is especially effective on exposed launch sites or during tethering.

Controls

With all that hot air making the balloon so buoyant, it would be extremely vulnerable at the point of landing if you didn't have some effective means of venting it quickly in order to deflate the envelope. The early hot-air fliers took a leaf out of the gas balloonists' book and installed once-only rip panels, but

these often involved a fiddly pre-flight ritual of preparing the rip-lock mechanisms. Nowadays, the most common method is the 'parachute valve' – a circular hole at the top or 'crown' of the balloon, which is sealed in flight by a slightly larger circle of fabric, the 'parachute'. The vertical load tapes at the top of the envelope come together and are attached to a crown-ring, usually of metal, and the parachute is held against these by the internal pressure of the hot air and by several positioning lines within the top of the envelope. During inflation with the envelope on its side the parachute is secured in place by a series of Velcro tabs – *see* Chapter 6. In flight the 'chute' can be opened slightly to release a little air to bring the balloon down or to halt an ascent, and upon landing it can be opened fully, which is especially important to stop the balloon dragging along the ground in faster wind speeds. To operate a conventional parachute valve a single red line comes down the inside of the envelope to the basket. On more elaborate systems there may be other colour-coded control lines. It is very easy for these lines to become over-cooked during the inflation and any damage should be quickly attended to. Trying to land a balloon without a functioning parachute valve would be an extremely tricky operation.

It is a simple and effective system, and one that allows very accurate and responsive control of the balloon. In recent years several variations on the theme have been developed to improve deflation upon landing, in particular for large passenger-carrying balloons. Nowadays you are unlikely to encounter rip panels except on some specially-shaped balloons where a conventional parachute valve would not be adequate. Some advertising balloons and just about all passenger balloons also feature side vents that are designed to rotate the balloon in flight. These usually take the form of slits high in the sides of the envelope – again held in place by internal pressure – and they have their own colour-coded control lines coming to the basket.

Burners and Fuel Systems
The modern balloon burner is a marvel of applied technology. Ballooning manuals published in the early days give dire warnings of pilot lights going out, of insufficient power resulting in unintentional contact with the ground or trees and other obstacles, and describe the extraordinary spectacle of a running take-off, where the poor crew was somehow persuaded to carry the inflated balloon and run downwind with it until it had become sufficiently pressurized. By contrast the modern burner is, if anything, too powerful.

The manufacturers all have their own

variation on the basic configuration and some burners will be triangular or square instead of circular. But they all work on the same principle. Liquid propane is forced from the fuel tanks or 'flight cylinders' up the pipes under its own pressure to the blast valve, which controls its flow into the coils of the burner. These encircle the flame and the heat of the flame vaporizes the propane, which then emerges from jets at the base of the burner and is ignited by a pilot light. Beautifully simple and scorchingly powerful with a typical double burner putting out a staggering 24 million BTU (British Thermal Units – 1BTU being the heat required to raise the temperature of 1lb of water by 1°F).

There is unfortunately a penalty for all this unadulterated power – hot-air balloon burners are noisy. The manufacturers have done much to improve the situation, for example by increasing the number of jets, but noise is a simple by-product of burner efficiency. Apart from it interrupting your most scintillating conversations at 2,000ft, this noise can upset animals. Dogs in particular seem to hear us coming miles ahead – probably something to do with the frequency of the sound. To alleviate the problem, most burners, if not all of them, are equipped with a secondary blast-valve, which bypasses the coils and burns neat liquid propane. Known variously as a 'whisper' or 'cow' burner, these produce an appreciably quieter sound and a much softened initial ignition noise as well as a more feathery flame profile. Of course, the manufacturers insist that these whisper burners produce the same output for the same fuel consumption as the main burners, but on behalf of the balloonists I would have to say that the jury is still out on that one.

One final observation on the subject of burners and their controls: there is as yet no standardization of the shape, position or size of the control handles. Get into one make of balloon and the main blast-valve handle might be plain metal while the whisper is ribbed and coloured red, but on another make of burner the blast valve will be red and the whisper blue. It's not unlike getting into a strange car and washing the windscreen when you really meant to indicate a left turn, but with a balloon the consequences can be more than just embarrassing. Ultimately there is only one adage to cover such situations and it should be engraved on every balloonist's skull: *familiarize yourself with the controls before you fly an unfamiliar balloon.*

Baskets

It's a lucky accident for ballooning that while modern technology has been applied to the fabrics and the burner, no one has been able to improve on the trusty old wicker basket and it has remained almost unchanged for over two centuries, a sturdy and resilient compartment for the pilot,

Nobody has been able to improve upon the traditional wicker basket.

passengers and the flight cylinders, that still manages to evoke the charms of a former age. Fibreglass, nylon and other man-made materials have been tried and found

Weaving a larger-sized basket around a tubular-steel frame.

wanting as none of them can soak up the punishment of repeated balloon landings without bending or cracking – whereas wicker absorbs the bangs and bounces back into shape.

Baskets are still made of willow or more commonly a combination of stripped cane and willow. Some manufacturers offer baskets with a solid marine-ply floor while others give the option of either a wooden or woven floor. Beneath the floor are hardwood runners, sometimes nylon edged for added protection for the bottom of the basket when it is being dragged upon landing.

Although balloon baskets are designed to flex under impact, a tubular-steel frame is incorporated for extra strength and to prevent distortion.

The wires coming down from the envelope, known as 'flying wires', are connected directly to the corners of the burner frame using kara-biners and to the steel 'basket' wires passing down through the basket and up the other side to form a secure cradle. To hold the burner in place, flexible nylon poles known as 'flexi-rigids' are slotted into each corner of the basket and into the burner frame. These are not structural as their main purpose is to prevent the burner continuing downwards on to the occupants' heads upon landing.

There is a simple step-hole in at least one side of most baskets and pairs of smaller holes in the four corners allow straps to pass through to hold the fuel cylinders in position inside.

The shape and size of balloon baskets vary enormously and many first-time fliers are surprised by how low the top edge of the average sports balloon basket can be – especially if you are quite tall. Some have curving sides swooping up to the corners to give added protection to the top of the fuel cylinders. Passenger balloon baskets tend to have much higher sides and additional internal partitioning to provide security and protection on landing. A handful of baskets

A standard medium-sized basket with twin burners and incorporating the sponsor's logo applied to the wickerwork.

exist that have been specially designed with a side door to provide wheelchair access for the disabled and these usually incorporate viewing panels in the sides.

As well as mere size there are other variations on the basket theme. In the USA the FireFly company has made a virtue of the triangular basket, complete with triangular burner frames, by stashing the tanks out of harm's way in the three corners. And there have been several attempts to create small and even foldable baskets for the much-travelled aeronaut who wants to get about without the inconvenience of bulky gear. American Brian Boland is a past master at this sort of ballooning innovation and his

A massive twenty-four-person basket built for a Swedish balloon ride operator.

lightweight balloons and baskets can be just about reduced to the size of hand baggage for international travel.

If you are feeling adventurous enough you can go one step further and dispose of the basket altogether. Once described as 'a balloon with a pair of braces', the one-man Cloudhopper has become a firm favourite for many pilots who enjoy the experience of riding in an armchair strapped directly to a fuel cylinder. They are great fun, although a little unsociable perhaps. But a word of caution to the new balloonist tempted by this route: it is possible to learn to fly with a hopper although it is inevitably a more difficult task, and in the UK your licence is only valid for this sort of balloon until you check-out on the more conventional version.

Care and Maintenance

As an aircraft there is only so much work that the owner can carry out on their balloon, although there are many aspects of maintenance and storage that will help to keep the equipment in the best of conditions. In the past some pilots have been tempted to make their own little amendments or alterations to the fuel systems and these are known to have contributed to fatal accidents. Look after your balloon and equipment responsibly and it will look after you.

Surprisingly perhaps, with the envelope there is a degree of permissible damage. This may sound alarming and new passengers can get somewhat nervous when they see unsightly burn holes around the mouth of a balloon. However, these do not affect the

One solution to the problem of wheelchair access to enable the less able to experience the joys of ballooning.

The Cloudhopper – no basket, just a tank, a harness and a small seat with the burner controls situated in the handles.

structural integrity of the envelope or its ability to contain hot air. Small holes can be patched using special self-adhesive mending tape made of balloon fabric. But if there is any damage above the first horizontal load tape (or approximately 15ft up from the mouth) the balloon should not be flown, and damage to any load-bearing parts such as the load tapes or wires, control lines or fuel systems is likewise unacceptable. Such repair work must be carried out by the manufacturer or an approved repair station and it must be signed-off by an approved Inspector.

The greatest threat to envelope fabric is mould or mildew, which can be caused if it is packed away damp or wet. Even packing a damp crownline, the rope from the top of the balloon, on an otherwise dry envelope has been known to cause this. It is a problem

that was virtually unheard of in the very early days, but some of the protective fabric coatings introduced in the 1980s seem to provide a breeding ground for this sort of growth. The first indication that your envelope has been infected is a bad musty smell when you inflate it and you may also be able to see some patchy mould or little clusters of black mildew spots. While it might not be very pretty, there is no evidence that it will affect a balloon's flying performance. To avoid mould and mildew it is crucial to always ensure that a balloon is dry when it is packed away. Easier said than done of course, especially in the winter, but if an envelope has to be packed away wet you should get it out within a few days and dry it off, either by cold inflating the envelope

American Brian Boland is a leading exponent of experimental ballooning and here he demonstrates his foldaway 'hand-luggage' basket.

or laying it out and letting evaporation get to work. If it is raining outside then a large sports hall or other building may be needed for the task – not to mention a team of volunteers.

If your envelope gets just plain dirty, which is especially noticeable on white or lighter-coloured balloons – perhaps from landing in mud or even animal muck – there are several proprietary brands of special balloon detergents on the market which, the manufacturers promise us, have been formulated not to damage the fabric's coatings in any way. But it is a laborious and difficult task to clean a balloon in this way and you still have to dry it out afterwards. Fortunately most dirt tends not to stick to

the modern balloon fabrics and such extreme measures are seldom necessary.

Damage to the control lines and all lines to the parachute valve are not acceptable and should be rectified immediately. The main control lines have a core of Kevlar, which is immensely strong, but if the outer covering becomes flame damaged it must be repaired or replaced. Similarly any leaks on the burner or fuel system must be dealt with immediately. If you discover any such damage when you inflate you must not fly the balloon regardless of the embarrassment this may cause on the launch field at the time. Egg on face may be messy but it does not kill.

Baskets, on the whole, are the most robust

part of the balloon and can be expected to remain airworthy for at least twice the life expectancy of the envelope. Care must be taken to ensure that baskets are not stored wet – either from standing in a puddle on a wet trailer or because of a muddy or wet landing site. Strong hide protects the bottom edges of a balloon basket, but if this becomes damp or wet over any length of time it will become soft and consequently more prone to further damage or mould. It is also very easy to get mud stuck within the weave of the basket and it must be carefully removed because if it is left there it will hold in the dampness and can cause the hide and wicker-work to rot.

Some manufacturers advocate an occasional extra coat of protective varnish for the basket, but there are opposing views on the wisdom of this as certain experts say that the varnish might simply serve to hold in any dampness if it is already present. Just as with the rest of the balloon and equipment, a vigilant eye, good house-keeping practices and an occasional spring-clean will extend the basket's life, improve your safety, and help to maintain the balloon's value.

4 Equipment

INFLATION FANS

Before the arrival of the inflation fan the method of inflating a hot-air balloon was an exhausting and faintly ludicrous operation involving much energetic flapping of the mouth to capture a bubble of air and some poor volunteer from the crew – appropriately dubbed 'Cremation Charlie' – going inside and holding the fabric up with a long broom! Needless to say the result was frequently a singed balloon and occasionally a slightly

An inflation fan fills the envelope with cold air before the burners can get to work.

singed Charlie. Tell this to the new balloonists and they think you must be pulling their leg.

The inflation fan couldn't have come along a moment too soon and now it is the universal means of filling the envelope with cold air before the burners are switched on. Most fans are fitted with petrol engines, in various sizes and outputs to suit the situation, which drive a wooden propeller protected by a wire-mesh cage. A 5hp (horse-power) fan is adequate for most smaller balloons whereas 8hp or more is needed for the bigger ones. It is not uncommon on the commercial show circuit or with pleasure flight operations to use two fans, one either side of the basket. The space a fan occupies in your trailer can also be a factor when choosing the right one.

Inflation fans are simple to use and have only four basic controls: an on/off switch, fuel supply switch, choke and throttle. There are some minor variations on their basic design; some fans are squatter and angled upwards while others stand more vertically, and to increase output some manufacturers have increased the number of fan blades from two to three. A marvellous aid to the balloonist, the fan is also a source of potential danger on the launch field if used incorrectly, if not in good repair, or if it becomes the subject of attention from over-curious spectators – so treat inflation fans with caution. Never try to move the fan while it is running and always ensure that the ignition switch and petrol flow are switched off at all times when not in use.

It is worth noting that some fans can only be moved by someone who is standing in front of the blades while others can be moved from behind, often by pushing down a brake mechanism which presses against the wheels to prevent the vibrating fan from 'walking' while it is operating. It is not unusual in the heat of the moment to see an inexperienced crew member, or well-intentioned bystander, attempting to move an operating fan, perhaps to avoid a tangle with the wires. I have even seen someone trying to lift one off the ground only for them to discover the huge power of the whirling propeller blades as it almost pulled them off their feet. So I leave it to you to decide which is the safer alternative – one you can move from behind, away from the propeller, or one where you have to stand in front of it.

Fans are surprisingly expensive, and by their nature very mobile, so take the trouble to engrave or mark them with some sort of identification to discourage their removal, no matter how unintentional.

INSTRUMENTS

While it is perfectly possible to fly a balloon without any instruments at all, in most situations they provide vital information for the pilot, and while some are essential others are considered to be optional. There are several instruments which the balloonist might make use of in flight:

- Altimeter – indicates height or altitude.
- Variometer – indicates vertical ascent or descent.
- Thermistor – internal envelope temperature at the crown.
- A watch.
- Compass.
- GPS (Global Positioning System).

Altimeter
An altimeter is basically a barometer that indicates an aircraft's height (and, yes, a balloon is an aircraft) above a particular

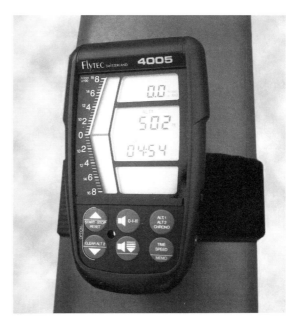

A modern strap-on instrument pack, which combines altimeter with variometer, temperature gauge and stopwatch.

reference point – usually sea level, or the elevation of the launch site. To avoid confusion 'height' is defined as the vertical distance above the ground, while 'altitude' is the distance above the mean sea level (amsl). They are *not* the same thing.

All altimeters work by indicating changes in air pressure on the assumption that this reduces at a steady rate with height. The older mechanical models did this by means of an aneroid capsule, which expanded or contracted with changes in air pressure at different heights. These movements were transmitted via a system of levers to move a needle (or up to three needles on some models to indicate hundreds, thousands and tens of thousands of feet) within the dial.

These mechanical instruments have largely gone out of fashion – although they work very well and do not require any batteries. They have been replaced with the modern electronic versions, usually combining the altimeter with the function of the variometer in a small lightweight unit that is easily mounted at eye-level on the basket uprights using Velcro straps. A tiny electronic sensor measures the pressure changes and displays these as readings on a Liquid Crystal Display (LCD). They are extremely accurate and at the press of a button most can be converted from feet to metres.

As all altimeters function by measuring the atmospheric pressure, which changes constantly from day to day or even from hour to hour, they can be adjusted or reset with a specific pressure setting as the reference point. In addition, to ensure that all aircraft are working to the same reference point, the UK is divided into pressure areas and individual airfields will also have their own localized pressure settings. But more on this in Chapter 5 under pre-flight preparations.

An altimeter is required by law to be carried on all flights.

Variometer
The companion to the altimeter is the variometer. Also working from changes in air pressure, this instruments indicates the rate of ascent and descent – the rise and fall – of the balloon. The mechanical 'varios' did this using a container of air with a very fine orifice. As the air pressure increased, air passed in through this orifice and as atmospheric pressure reduced, it flowed out, to be measured by a sensitive airflow-measuring device which moved a needle up or down. These instruments were incredibly sensitive and would even react if carried up or down a staircase, though the changes in pressure must have been tiny. (Tell me of one pilot who hasn't tried this the day their new instruments arrived!)

The electronic vario uses the same pressure sensors as the electronic altimeter with the addition of an integrator circuit to give the rate of change. This information is displayed on the LCD in either a graphic form, with dial or scale, and/or figures. These modern instruments are very reliable and quite reasonably priced, and many also feature various audio warning options. They either give an almost continuous whistle or whine that changes pitch as the rate of climb changes, or they can sound an alarm when a given rate is exceeded. The former can become irritating during the course of a flight, but the latter is a useful reminder if the pilot has become too engrossed in map reading or chatting to the passengers.

It is not uncommon during flight training for the instructor to turn the instruments off or move them out of view of the PuT as it is all too easy for the newcomer to become transfixed by every little change on the display. (This even happens with some passengers who become compelled to relay the readings out loud!) It is far better to 'get your eye in' rather than rely too much on the instruments at this early stage.

Some smaller instrument packs, aimed primarily at mountaineers or hang-glider fliers, are adequate for a balloonist's needs, but the wristwatch types are really not sensitive enough. Penny-pinching on instruments is always going to be a false economy.

Thermistor
The thermistor, or 'pyrometer' as it is sometimes called, measures the temperature at the top of the balloon. A small sensor is located inside the envelope near the crown, and connected via a thin wire or radio signal to a readout in the basket. There are two schools of thought regarding thermistors: in general most hot-air balloons are heated within a healthy safety margin and in theory, provided that the correct load calculations have been made and the balloon does not exceed the anticipated flight parameters, thermistors are not essential for the ordinary balloonist. However, I know of some pilots who almost fly by them, judging when to

As GPSs have got smaller over the years, so too have the prices.

burn by the temperature on the readout, and for ballooning in more extreme circumstance – such as very high altitude flights or perhaps when operating in hotter climates – a thermistor is vital.

A Watch
Arguably the single most important instrument of them all, a watch provides the means of monitoring the rate of fuel consumption and is essential in all navigational calculations. Never fly without one, as a watch or timepiece is the only other instrument required by law on all flights.

Compass
They are so small and light that all balloon pilots should keep a compass in their pocket at all times. It is not uncommon for balloons to rotate in flight and many a PuT, and for that matter qualified pilot, has become disoriented at some time. Having said

that, the GPS has taken over many functions of the compass, if not all of the other instruments.

When using a compass on the ground make sure that you stand a little away from any large metallic objects, such as the retrieve vehicle, as they could influence the position of its needle.

GPS
The Global Positioning System is one of the technological marvels of modern times. Originally devised by the US military, GPS can calculate your position to an incredible degree of accuracy by taking fixes from a network of satellites. Not surprisingly, the system was quickly adopted by aviators and, although the early units were bulky, the latest models are about the size of a mobile phone and, as with most embryonic technology, the prices have come right down.

Airband radio with optional handheld microphone.

So what will the GPS do for you? As well as indicating your exact location it will give your speed relative to the ground and the direction in which you are going, plus your altitude (although this does not take into account the need for using specified pressure settings as with the altimeter). Depending on which model you choose the display might be as figures and/or graphics, and most will include a map function either moving with you or showing your movement. Some have their own built-in airspace database which displays information for anywhere in the world. It is also possible to enter 'way points' or targets and their relative position will be constantly updated. But perhaps the most useful function of the GPS is that it can provide a reliable record of your flight with

positions and heights all mapped out, and linkable to your computer at home.

There is, however, one very important footnote on the GPS. They are not accepted by national aviation authorities as the sole means of navigation. This is because they rely on an external source of information and on occasion the US military has suspended the system, or it may be that in certain situations an adequate satellite fix is not available.

RADIOS

Most balloonists prefer the modern handheld airband radios, which have a variety of functions including programmable channels and a readout on the LCD. These radios have a more than adequate range for most ballooning situations, but as they work on line-of-sight the quality of reception can diminish behind hills or among buildings. I would recommend always carrying a spare and fully charged NiCad (Nickel Cadmium) battery to ensure no unwanted loss of radio contact mid-flight. It always happens at the most inconvenient moment.

In most countries balloonists have a dedicated radio frequency, but correct radio procedure should still be observed at all times to ensure efficient communication and to prevent the airwaves becoming clogged up with chit-chat. Licensing requirements may vary from country to country. In the UK the operator of an airband radio requires an RT (Radiotelephony) licence, and the radio set itself and even the base-station fitted in the retrieve vehicle require the purchase of an annual licence.

Note that it is illegal to use mobile phones in *any* aircraft.

PILOT'S FLIGHT BAG

One final and important piece of equipment is the pilot's flight bag, which should contain the maps, compass, documents including insurance documents, your licences and pilot's log book (although the balloon's log book is best left in the retrieve in case of total loss as it is the only record of the last inspection, modifications or repairs, and the hours flown) plus additional sources of ignition. The pilot lights on the modern burners seldom go out, but it would be a foolish pilot who didn't carry alternatives to the built-in piezo igniters and I always fly with a hand-held gas lighter (designed for gas cookers), a welder's sparker *and* several boxes of matches. Between flights the instruments, gloves, radios and so on can all be stored in this one place and are far less likely to be left behind.

FIRE AND FIRST AID

Fire extinguishers and first-aid kits are only mandatory for passenger balloons in the UK, but all balloonists are strongly advised to carry them, and most manufacturers supply these as part of a new balloon's equipment.

More information on the different types of fire extinguishers and their use is given in Chapter 9 on dealing with propane fires.

Typical off-the-shelf first-aid pack.

Few of the standard first-aid kits make much provision for the treatment of burns, even though this is potentially a high-risk injury associated with our activities. So it is worth spending a little extra and adding items to the basic kit. Don't forget that most of the contents of a first-aid kit will have an expiry date printed on the individual packaging and this validity should be regularly checked.

5 Preflight Preparation

GET MET

Before the start of any balloon flight it is essential that the pilot obtains accurate weather information and understands how this directly affects the decision whether to fly or not and the choice of launch site. In the broadest terms good flyable conditions might be wind speeds around 5 to 8kt on the surface, up to 15kt or so at 2,000ft, reasonably good visibility and no rain. That is not to say that balloons can't be flown in higher wind speeds if a pilot feels comfortable with their own level of experience and flying skills. Many balloonists feel that if they can stand the balloon upright at the launch site then conditions are probably okay, but above 10kt on the surface that is likely to be increasingly difficult.

Nowadays, when it comes to obtaining a forecast, balloonists are faced with a bewildering number of sources of weather information, although some might say that their increased volume is at the expense of accuracy. Most pilots begin with the TV weather forecast to obtain an overview of the situation. After that it is a matter of personal preference and sometimes expense in choosing the source of more specific aviation related information which falls into two categories: *forecasts* of expected weather conditions, and *reports* of actual weather.

The Met Office issues AIRMETs, intended specifically for pilots, four times daily and these divide the country into three large areas – Scottish Region, Northern Region and Southern – with additional, smaller forecast areas for the busy Southeast, Southwest and Cross Channel areas. This information

Dodging powerful cu-nimbs in Antigua.

is available by telephone, through the METFAX fax service or via the Internet (*see* Further Information). For fax or Internet users the information is available in several different forms with either a written area forecast, a UK low-level forecast chart or a UK spot winds chart. AIRMET Aerodrome Forecasts (TAFs) and Actual Weather Reports (METARs) are provided for around 100 aerodromes in the UK – again available by telephone, fax or Internet. But these are only of use if you are going to be flying in their vicinity and in some areas the designated aerodromes are few and far between. All AIRMET information is supplied in specific formats and an explanation of these and the abbreviations used is available from the Met Office.

In addition to AIRMET there are several commercial weather forecasting services and some of these will even provide a forecaster to talk to you on the telephone to give information for your area and to answer your questions, although this can be costly and the quality of the information provided often depends on the individual forecaster's understanding of the specific needs of balloonists and your locality. Alternatives include the more general telephone or fax weather information lines, automated weather station services, and many of the regional balloon groups, which now pool their resources to provide an information service to their members.

For most balloonists it soon becomes second nature to always keep one eye on the weather and to constantly monitor developments.

For the purpose of preflight procedures we will concentrate on the specific weather information needed. When obtaining this it is important to keep a written record, and using a standard form, such as the Met Form devised by the BBAC, helps to ensure that nothing is missed out. Here are the main areas specified:

- Forecast area.
- Period of forecast.
- General synoptic situation.
- Winds – direction and speeds on the surface and upper levels and their trend.
- Temperatures.
- Cloud – type, amount, base and tops.
- Surface visibility.
- Remarks, warnings, thermal activity, etc.
- QNH – the barometric pressure.
- Sunrise or sunset times.
- Further outlook.
- Source of information and time of issue.

It looks like a long list so let's look at each of these headings in more detail to determine their relevance.

Forecast Area

This may be specified as the launch site and surrounding area – an average balloon flight covers anything between five and fifteen miles, but as some sources of weather information might cover half the country in one broad forecast it is important to ensure that the information you obtain does apply to your flight area. Be prepared to go to the launch site and assess the local weather conditions for yourself. And remember that just because an official forecast says it will be flyable doesn't necessarily make it so.

Period of Forecast

Specify the time period concerned. It is worth noting that virtually all official sources of aeronautical weather information are based on UTC (also known as 'Zulu') which is the same as Greenwich Mean Time (GMT).

General Synoptic Situation

Gives a broad overview of the weather situation. Perhaps high or low pressure dominates the area, or a cold front is coming in from the west for example. Atmospheric stability is usually covered here.

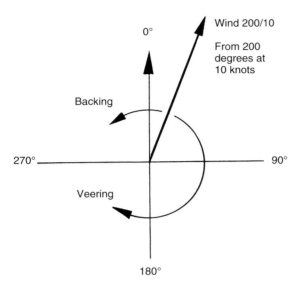

Wind 200/10

From 200 degrees at 10 knots

Wind directions.

Winds

The term wind simply refers to the movement of air over the Earth's surface. For aviation purposes wind strength is given in knots (kt), which is speed measured in nautical miles per hour. A nautical mile (nm) equals 1.15 statute miles and so a speed expressed as 10kt is going to be faster than one which is 10mph. Non-aeronautical weather forecasts are often the first recourse for the balloonist and as they are intended for the layman the wind speed is invariably expressed in miles per hour.

Wind direction is always given as the direction *from* which it is coming and is expressed as degrees of a 360-degree clockwise circle with north at the top at 0 degrees or 360 degrees. Near the surface the wind is affected by various geographical features and as a result is described in only vague terms such as a 'westerly' (coming *from* the west), or a 'northwesterly' (*from* the northwest). At height the wind direction becomes a little more consistent and can be specified in degrees, and when direction and strength

are described together they may be written as 270/35 – coming from 270 degrees at a speed of 35kt.

A wind that is shifting in a clockwise direction on the 360-degree scale is described as 'veering', and an anti-clockwise change as 'backing'. Therefore, a wind that has moved round from 270 to 360 is veering, while one moving from 180 to 120 is said to have backed.

In some forecasts intended for sailors the wind speed is given as a Beaufort Scale number. This scale, from Force 1 up to Force 12, is a means of estimating wind speed by reference to the appearance of the sea with Force 1 'Light air' indicating an average speed of 2kt, Force 2 'Light breeze' at 5kt and so on up to Force 12 which is a full-blown hurricane blowing at speeds above 65kt!

The PuT must learn to judge the wind speeds both on the surface and at height. In general ballooning terms 0–5kt on the surface is considered to be calm or slow, 6–10kt is moderate and 11–15kt is fast. There are many wind-measuring instruments available on the market and these operate with varying degrees of accuracy, but it is far better to learn to judge it for yourself. Keep an eye on the treetops for lower levels, and watch any cloud movement or release a small helium-filled toy balloon to get an idea of how the upper air currents are behaving. Look in particular for gusts or any indications that the wind speed or direction might be changing.

No instructor or examiner is going to condemn a trainee pilot who decides to cancel a flight on site because the conditions are not suitable. And while it is good for the PuT to experience a wide range of conditions during their training period it can be very demoralizing if the instructor has to take over the landing because it has become too fast. An examiner may also cancel a check flight if the wind speed is too slow for the required flight exercises to be carried out. A balloonist has to learn to be philosophical because sometimes you just can't win with the weather, and no amount of wishing otherwise will make one ounce of difference.

Temperatures

The surface temperature is required in order to make the loading calculations. Forecasts may also give anticipated temperatures alongside wind information for the higher levels – always in degrees Celsius.

Cloud

The different types of cloud are discussed further in Chapter 12 and for the purposes of Met information there are specific ways to describe them. For example, puffy cumulus clouds are described as 'Cu', a layer of these as stratocumulus or 'Sc' and a continuous layer of stratus or flatter clouds as 'St'. Perhaps the worst form of cloud for the balloonist is the tall cumulonimbus known variously as a 'CuNb' or 'cu-nimb' or just 'CB' – a storm cloud which can generate hazardous flying conditions with powerful vertical and horizontal air currents, not to mention thunder and lightning.

The amount of cloud is known as the 'cover' and this can be measured by roughly dividing the sky visually into eighths or 'oktas'. Cloud cover of 1/8 is described as few, 2–3 as scattered, 4–7 broken and 8/8 as overcast.

The height at which clouds begin to form is known as their 'base'. And a low base, at 1,500ft or less for example, will compromise visibility to such an extent that the flight will have to be cancelled.

Surface Visibility

Horizontal visibility is vital for any aircraft to be seen and for the pilot to see others. No balloonist should ever launch into fog or if they expect fog to occur. Visibility is usually expressed in kilometres, except when less than 5km when metres are used instead.

Visual Meteorological Conditions (VMC) are defined in the Air Navigation Order (the ANO) which is the definitive reference for all UK aviation law, and below 3,000ft above ground level (agl) a balloon should have a flight visibility of 1,500m, be clear of cloud and in sight of the surface (*see* Chapter 12).

Remarks, Warnings, etc

Apart from the obvious perils of thunderstorms, warnings may cover the development of showers or a lowering of the cloud base. On morning flights in the summer there is also the risk of convection or thermic activity as the warmth of the sun begins to have an effect, and this can be quite severe on a hot day. *See* Chapter 12 for more on this.

QNH – The Barometric Pressure

Back to the altimeter. As mentioned before, the pressure setting on the instruments can be adjusted to allow for barometric pressure changes from day to day or even hour to hour. There is also the 'Q' system, which exists to ensure that fliers are operating to specific or agreed pressure settings.

QNH is the more commonly used pressure setting for ballooning purposes as it makes the instruments read the balloon's altitude. Its value varies with changes in the atmospheric pressure and because these can be considerable from one end of the country to the other the UK is divided into 'pressure areas' each with its own regional QNH. The significance of QNH is that it gives an altitude reading that directly relates to the maps we use, although these are sometimes marked in metres whereas we are flying in feet. Deduct the height of any feature on the map from your altitude and the result is, approximately, your height.

One way to obtain an unofficial version of QNH at launch is to consult the map for the elevation above mean sea level (amsl) of the launch site and to adjust the pressure setting until the altimeter's reading matches it. But always bear in mind that the accuracy will change with any subsequent variations in atmospheric pressure and this can occur during the duration of a balloon flight.

When flying within controlled airspace a QNH setting will be specified by the Air Traffic Controllers (ATC) to ensure safe separation of all aircraft.

QFE is the pressure setting in millibars that makes the altimeter read the height above a particular reference point. This is most commonly used in the fixed-wing world where an incoming pilot will request the aerodrome QFE by radio and this will give the height reading above that aerodrome's runway level. As a result, as the wheels of the plane touch down on the runway the instruments should read zero feet.

There is one setting that does not change. The international pressure setting that defines 'Flight Levels' is 1013.2mb. These are a series of levels at higher altitudes and they are expressed in hundreds of feet on the 1013.2 setting. For example, with the altimeter reading 6,500ft the aircraft is at Flight Level 65 (FL 65). While the actual height might vary to a degree with the changes in atmospheric pressure the important thing is that all aircraft and ATCs are operating to the same and agreed setting.

Sunrise or Sunset Times
These can alter considerably during the year (at a rate of approximately two minutes every day) or at different locations either east to west of course, but also with latitude, and in the summer the north of England or Scotland can enjoy more hours of daylight than the south. Apart from the obvious importance of being able to see where you are going during your flight, there are also legal definitions for daylight – with 'day' officially beginning half an hour before sunrise, and 'night' half an hour after sunset. Although it is legal to fly until dusk, it is advisable to

plan for flights to end before sunset to allow for a healthy safety margin. It also makes the retrievers' job a little easier.

Further Outlook
It is always a good idea to have some idea of what the weather will be doing later in the day or the following day. If the wind speed is perhaps marginal then the forecast may indicate whether the trend is for it to increase or decrease. It also helps to plan ahead for the next flight.

Source of Information and Time of Issue
Always record the source of any weather information and the time when it was issued.

Expected Track of the Balloon
Armed with the Met information and knowing the likely direction or 'track' that the balloon will take, it is time to assess the suitability of the launch site. Is it possible to fly from that location without encountering physical obstacles or controlled airspace on the way? And are there suitable landing sites downwind, namely in the direction the wind is taking the balloon?

LOAD CALCULATIONS

It is almost time to get our hands on the balloon equipment, but there is one final preparation to be made – the load calculation.

Before every flight the all-up weight of the balloon must be calculated to ensure that it is flown within safe limits. An over-laden balloon can easily become overheated. I know of one celebrated case where a pilot just couldn't bring himself to say no to additional passengers to such an extent that the top of his balloon started coming apart when he tried to get airborne. That is an extreme example, but it is vital for your safety, if not for the longevity of your balloon, to ensure that proper load calculations are made first.

Load calculation chart.

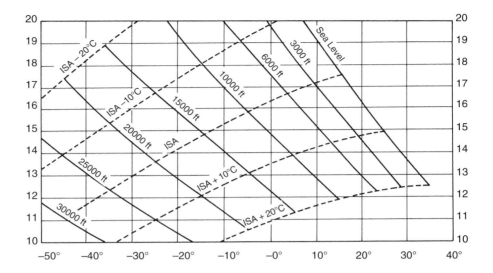

And it isn't as difficult as it might at first appear.

The amount a balloon can lift is dependent on the ambient temperature and the altitude at which it is to be flown, and the loading chart is used to make the calculations.

The horizontal scale gives ambient air temperature in °C, and the vertical scale is the available load (or gross lift) at an envelope temperature of 100°C.

Start by locating the actual temperature of the day at the launch site along the bottom line. Follow this vertically until it crosses one of the diagonal lines corresponding with the altitude of the launch site. For most flights in the UK this roughly corresponds to sea level, but in many parts of the world this might be several thousands of feet higher. From this intersection move horizontally to the vertical scale to read off the available gross lift per 1,000cu ft volume at the launch site.

To take into account the fall in temperature and air pressure with altitude in order to calculate the gross lift at a given altitude, go back to the point of intersection on the sea-level line and, running parallel to the dotted lines, trace a slightly curving line down towards the bottom left of the chart until you meet the required line of altitude. From this intersection go horizontally for the gross lift at that altitude, or vertically downwards for the expected temperature. Bear in mind that the dotted lines on the chart only indicate the way the International Standard Atmosphere (ISA) should behave and it is important to mark your own line in parallel for your particular calculation.

The ready reckoner illustrated over the page refers to different sizes of balloons and will quickly give a total figure for the available gross lift, at sea level or at the altitude you intend to fly. The disposable lift is this figure minus the balloon's empty weight – with no occupants or fuel – which is to be found in each balloon's log book. Make sure that the combined weight of the passengers, fuel and other items of personal equipment does not exceed this available or disposable lift.

It should be noted that for any flights higher than normal operational limits, the ISA may not be a sufficiently accurate guide and more precise Met information will be required to produce an accurate indication of lift. An overall limit of 20lb per 1,000ft is imposed to prevent excessive loading at low

Lift per 1000 cu. ft	BALLOON SIZE																			
	20	31	42	56	65	77	84	90	105	120	133	140	145	160	180	210	250	300	375	500
10	200	315	420	560	650	775	840	900	1050	1200	1330	1400	1450	1600	1800	2100	2500	3000	3750	5000
11	220	346	462	616	715	852	924	990	1155	1320	1463	1540	1595	1760	1980	2310	2750	3300	4125	5500
12	240	378	504	672	780	930	1008	1080	1260	1440	1596	1680	1740	1920	2160	2520	3000	3600	4500	6000
13	260	409	546	728	845	1007	1092	1170	1365	1560	1729	1820	1885	2080	2340	2730	3250	3900	4875	6500
14	280	441	588	784	910	1085	1176	1260	1470	1680	1862	1960	2030	2240	2520	2940	3500	4200	5250	7000
15	300	472	630	840	975	1162	1260	1350	1575	1800	1995	2100	2175	2400	2700	3150	3750	4500	5625	7500
16	320	504	672	896	1040	1240	1344	1440	1680	1920	2128	2240	2320	2560	2880	3360	4000	4800	6000	8000
17	340	535	714	952	1105	1317	1428	1530	1785	2040	2261	2380	2465	2720	3060	3570	4250	5100	6375	8500
18	360	567	756	1008	1170	1395	1512	1620	1890	2160	2394	2520	2610	2880	3240	3780	4500	5400	6750	9000
19	380	598	798	1064	1235	1472	1596	1710	1995	2280	2527	2660	2755	3040	3420	3990	4750	5700	7125	9500
20	400	630	840	1120	1300	1550	1680	1800	2100	2400	2660	2800	2900	3200	3600	4200	5000	6000	7500	10000

TOTAL PERMITTED LIFT (lb)

Ready reckoner.

temperatures, and this is reduced even further on very large balloons. These charts do not take into account those situations when the temperature actually increases with height – *see* 'Temperature Inversions' in Chapter 12.

But that's enough theory – let's get to the launch site.

6 Getting off the Ground

From the moment you arrive at the launch site until the time when the balloon gets airborne usually takes around forty-five minutes to an hour, and this chapter looks at the processes involved.

SELECTING A LAUNCH SITE

Pre-flight preparations completed, you are confident that the weather conditions are suitable for a flight and that your choice of launch-site location is appropriate for the anticipated direction the balloon will be going. In an ideal world the perfect launch site would be a grass field sheltered by trees, free of downwind obstacles and far away from any livestock. The soft tops of the trees serve to feather the air flow passing over them whereas buildings or other hard-edged forms of shelter can actually create pockets of 'curlover' and turbulent air.

In addition to the physical requirements, the pilot must have the permission of the landowner to use a launch site – an instructing pilot may ask to see a copy of written permission – and its proximity to any Sensitive Areas (*see* Chapter 8) must be taken into account. The choice of launch site must also comply with the requirements of Air Law (*see* Chapter 12). In some areas

The moment of lift-off.

Preparing to launch from an exposed launch site.

local balloon groups have established their own launch sites, but don't simply assume you also have a right to use them. Make sure you have gone through the proper channels first. One common misconception, excuse the pun, is that common land or public parks in the UK are free for anyone to use as they wish. In fact the use of many, if not all, will be strictly governed by local by-laws.

Once on the launch site the PuT is expected to have identified the wind direction on the surface and selected a suitable position for laying out the balloon. The weather forecast should provide some indication of the wind direction to be expected, but local influences can have their own effect. The best way to quickly check the wind conditions on site is to release a small helium-filled toy balloon (and in particular note what happens when it clears any shelter). Traditionally balloon pilots have tossed handfuls of dry grass into the air to observe the surface breeze. Another useful and extremely cheap wind indicator is a narrow strip of polythene approximately 5mm wide, cut from a thin plastic shopping bag, attached to the retrieve vehicle's aerial to serve as a windsock.

When selecting a position on the launch site to lay out the balloon it is tempting to head straight for the shelter of the trees, but while shelter may seem desirable in many ways it can also create its own problems. When a balloon lifts off from a sheltered site to enter a layer of faster moving air the effect on its curved upper surface acts like the curve of an aircraft's wing and additional aerodynamic lift will be created. That may sound desirable, but as soon as the balloon begins to move with that new airflow this lift, known wisely as 'false lift', will soon vanish and unwary pilots will find their balloons rapidly dropping back down to the ground. This effect can be verified by a simple experiment with a running tap and a spoon. Imagine that the column of water represents a flow of air and, holding the spoon vertically by the handle, allow the back of the rounded side to lightly touch the water. See for yourself what happens.

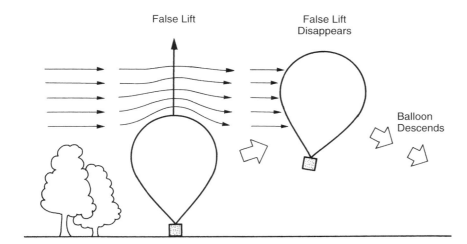

False Lift

False Lift
Disappears

Balloon
Descends

*Diagram showing
false lift.*

The other effect of launching from shelter is that the higher airflow is likely to have a cooling influence on the envelope and in more extreme conditions may even distort it, pushing out some of the air. It is essential, therefore, when taking off from shelter to have plenty of excess or spare lift. In calmer conditions shelter becomes much less of a consideration.

One last comment on the subject of trees: give yourself enough room. Balloons are big things and many an inexperienced pilot has stood their balloon up only to find that it is being poked at by the branches.

PREPARING FOR INFLATION

Every balloon comes with a manual supplied by the manufacturer that specifies the correct procedure for rigging the balloon and its inflation, but the following guide runs through the process in general terms.

Position on the launch field selected, it is time to unload the trailer. First off is the bottom end – the basket, cylinders and burners, and so on – which will have been disassembled for transportation. Occasionally some balloonists transport their baskets fully rigged with the burner in position, but in general this is not recommended by the manufacturers as continued and repetitive shaking in transit can eventually cause weaknesses in the welded joints on the burner frame.

The balloon is going to be laid out downwind so make sure that the basket is correctly oriented front to back. This may be obvious on some baskets with perhaps a foot step on the back for example, but on others it is sometimes difficult to tell the front from the back so don't be afraid to mark it in some way. A piece of coloured string might suffice.

With the basket in the upright position the pilot should check the fuel cylinder gauges to see that they are full and that the cylinders are secured and properly positioned so that they will be the right way up with the basket tipped over. (The reasons for this are discussed in Chapter 9 on propane and cylinders.) Four nylon poles, the flexi-rigids, slot into the top corners of the basket's frame and the burner frame sits on top of these, and this too needs to be correctly oriented with the dials reading the right way up when the basket is on its side. This can be especially important if your pilot lights work on vapour and not all your cylinders are equipped to supply it.

Assembling the equipment.

The basket wires are attached to the burner frame using the karabiners, and the fuel lines are positioned and attached to the flight cylinders. Padded pole-covers wrap around the flexi-rigid uprights to tidy away the wires and fuel lines.

Burner Test

With the basket still upright this is the best time to conduct a burner test. This simple but essential procedure is conducted to ensure that there is adequate fuel on board, it is at an acceptable pressure, it is not contaminated with water, and that the fuel system is delivering fuel without any problems or leaks. Some pilots are inclined to do this test later on when the inflation has been completed, but the drawback to this approach is that by then the inflated balloon is overhead and the passengers and crew are either in or surrounding the basket. It is far better to do it at this early stage, with only the pilot on board, and to make it part of your regular prelaunch preparations.

To conduct a burner test the appropriate valves on the flight cylinder are determined by whether your pilot light operates from the main liquid supply or requires a separate vapour supply (*see* Chapter 9). This sequence assumes the latter, but is easily adapted for liquid supplied pilot lights.

Burner Test Sequence

- Open liquid valve on the flight cylinder first: 'Lead with liquid'.
- Check for sound, smell or feel of leaks.
- Open the vapour (pilot-light) valve.
- Light pilot light.
- After checking that everyone is prepared for what comes next, operate blast valve.
- Close liquid valve at cylinder.
- Operate 'cow' burner to burn out the fuel line.
- Close vapour tap at cylinder.
- Observe burn out of pilot light.
- Switch off pilot valve at burner.
- Operate both blast and pilot light to ensure all supply of fuel is off and the hoses are empty.

It is a golden rule to never leave fuel in the system unnecessarily. Each cylinder should be tested in turn, and a fire extinguisher should be at hand at all times.

Low fuel pressure is a symptom of low winter temperatures and it can result in a less effective flame and poor flight control. In summer the fuel pressure is naturally around the 100psi (pounds per square inch) mark, but if the balloon is stored outside on a cold frosty night this can drop to a feeble 40psi. There are methods of boosting the pressure, either through warming the cylinders or by adding a top-up of nitrogen gas, and these procedures should be described in the balloon's manual. On no account should you be tempted to take the cylinders indoors overnight to keep them warm in front of the fire!

Note that the configuration of cylinder valves and the burner controls can vary from one manufacturer to another, and even from one balloon to another, so familiarize yourself with the manual before flying a particular balloon.

Burner tests completed, now is a good time to get all the equipment on board: maps, igniters, radios, instruments, fire extinguisher and first-aid box. Final checks of these will come later.

Laying Out

The basket is tipped over onto its side so that the envelope can be attached. Place the envelope bag approximately 15ft downwind of the burner frame and pull out the mouth of the balloon. The number of flying wires coming from the envelope to the attachment points on the corners of the burner frame will depend on the number of vertical load tapes on the envelope (a result of the number of gores). Some manufacturers colour code the ends of the wires into groups with plastic strips, which correspond to blue for the upper wires or 'sky', and black for the lower ones or 'ground' when the balloon is laid on the ground, but if in any doubt the best procedure is to start from scratch. Lay the

mouth on the ground the right way up – the scoop is at the bottom – and go round the mouth in a circle attaching the wires one at a time. With the wires attached the karabiners should be locked closed – close the screw gates by hand only and turn back (or undo) by a quarter rotation to prevent jamming under load. Personally I always advise my crew to lock the karabiners every single time they handle them. That way they are less likely to be forgotten and left unlocked. Should a balloon be stood up with a karabiner in the unlocked position it is virtually impossible to remedy the situation without deflating again, and the open karabiner is likely to have been irreversibly stretched. Some experts also suggest that karabiners should only be positioned with the gates downwards to prevent unscrewing.

A 2.5 tonne karibiner.

Now go back to the mouth and just run round it to check that the wires are not tangled or crossed over each other. Some pilots like to group each set of wires with their own karabiner and to coil them when they pack the balloon away, but this is generally advised against by the manufacturers as repeated tight coiling could kink or weaken the wires. The pilot will clip the ends of the control lines to the basket or burner frame. This is especially important with the red line to the parachute, in order to ensure that it is available and to hand at all times. It can be relocated later as part of the pre-flight checks if not conveniently placed.

Before going any further a restraint rope must be attached from the pair of karabiners on the burner frame's rear-facing corners to a secure towing point on the retrieve vehicle, which has been positioned with its front bumper a few feet upwind of the basket, parked in gear and the keys left with the vehicle! There are various simple quick-release mechanisms offered by the balloon manufacturers which all operate by pulling a handle which is secured during inflation by a safety pin. Never be tempted to do without a restraint rope even in the calmest of conditions.

Check

- Screw gates closed on karabiners.
- Red line to parachute valve attached.
- Quick release attached – at both ends!
- Vehicle is in gear, brake is on and the keys are in the ignition.
- All fuel valves closed and all fuel lines vented.

The envelope bag can now be dragged or carried downwind away from the basket, leaving the envelope trailing behind in a long sausage. Pulling only on the load tapes, passengers and crew are invited to help spread out the envelope sideways, although some pilots prefer to leave it to the inflation fan to do this job.

Before dealing with the pilot's actions during the inflation, it is important to make sure that the other people on the launch field, the ground crew and passengers, understand what is expected of them.

BRIEFING THE CREW

The envelope is now laid out like a vast balloon-shaped pancake, the equipment is in place and it is time for action. At this point, the launch site can become a noisy place and this sometimes makes communication difficult, so it is essential to ensure that all crew members or any recruited volunteers are properly briefed. For the crew there are two main areas of activity, at the crown of the balloon and at the mouth.

The aim of the two members of the mouth crew during the cold inflation is to position themselves either side of the mouth of the envelope and to hold it up as round and as open as possible to allow the fan to do its job pumping in the cold air. They should wear protective gloves – and if they are to be involved with the hot inflation they should cover any bare skin with natural fibre clothing. At all times they must keep their feet off and outside of the flying wires.

With the flaccid envelope filling out with cold air, the pilot, or a suitably experienced crew member, will go round to the top end of the balloon to position and attach the circular parachute valve into the opening using the small Velcro tabs. These are only there to hold the parachute in place during the inflation process, and they are usually numbered and/or colour coded to assist in positioning. Care must be taken to ensure that none of the load tapes at the crown or any of the internal parachute lines become tangled.

With the envelope now nicely rounded the pilot can make an internal inspection to

Crownline crew brace themselves for the moment of hot inflation.

check that the parachute is properly rigged and that the control lines and pulleys are all moving freely. Satisfied that everything is in order the hot inflation can begin, and once the burners are firing the balloon will stand upright surprisingly quickly.

The crownline, which is attached to the crown ring at the top of the balloon, serves to prevent the envelope from rising too rapidly and to steady it once it is in the upright position. The number of crew required to hold the crownline depends on the size of the balloon, but for most smaller balloons one person is usually adequate. It is important that the crownline crew refuses offers of additional help, no matter how well intentioned. Wearing thick leather gloves to protect their hands, they should hold the rope at its very end and resist any temptation to wrap it around their hands or body.

Getting the crown crew to hold the rope with the right amount of force at the right time can be frustrating, but if they are doing it wrong it is because the pilot has not briefed them adequately. During the cold inflation the rope should be held slack – pull too tight and there is a risk that the parachute will be pulled out and away from its Velcro attachments. Ideally the pilot should give a clear signal when he is ready to hot inflate, and once the burner noise is heard the crown crew needs to hold the rope taut and then keep pulling on it using all of their weight as the envelope starts to rise up – they shouldn't fight it because they won't win. Once the balloon is upright, the pilot should give a signal for the end of the rope to be brought to the basket. The crownline crew shouldn't dawdle at this stage, as the pilot might need their assistance around the basket.

With modern inflation fans filling the envelope so efficiently many pilots decide to do away with the mouth crew during the hot inflation. It is entirely optional, but if mouth crew are to assist they should position themselves with the Nomex protecting them from the heat of the flame and facing the pilot to watch for any signals. If they feel uncomfortable or in danger at any time they should let go of the mouth and move away. As with the

The burners are tilted upwards to blast hot-air into the mouth.

crown crew they should come to the basket when it is upright and apply some weight by leaning on the basket edge while keeping their feet firmly on the ground.

One golden rule applies to everyone at the launch site: *If for any reason your feet should leave the ground, let go immediately. Do not under any circumstances hold on.*

That leaves just the operation of the fan itself. This should be positioned beside the basket pointing into the mouth with the on/off switch facing towards the basket. But not with the blades directly in line with the pilot or bystanders in case bits from a broken or disintegrating blade start flying off. The role of the fan crew is to direct the airflow into the centre of the balloon's mouth. Most pilots will commence the hot inflation with the fan still running, perhaps on a reduced throttle setting, and once the envelope begins to lift the fan needs to be turned off – either by the pilot or by the crew at a pre-determined signal – and moved well out of the way of the basket.

Some pilots prefer to operate the fan themselves, but it is always useful to have a briefed crew member on hand in case the basket starts travelling sideways and knocks the fan over, risking fire from an oil or petrol spillage or possibly damaging the blades.

PASSENGER BRIEFING

There is one further briefing that should be conducted in the peace and calm before the noisy inflation begins – the passenger briefing. The best time for this is just after the burner test when the basket is still upright. Clear and simple instructions should be given to ensure that the passengers know:

- What is expected of them if helping during the inflation.
- How and when to enter the basket.
- What to do on landing.
- Not to interfere with any of the controls.
- Carriage of personal items and what to do with them on landing.
- What to do in the eventuality of pilot incapacity through illness.
- Disembarkation and actions after landing.

The essence of a good briefing is to communicate clearly. Try to avoid jargon or technical terms. Maintain eye contact throughout to ensure you have their attention, and demonstrate any postures or actions. Most first-time passengers will be a little nervous about the flight, so humour may be appropriate in lightening the atmosphere as long as it does not undermine the effectiveness of the briefing.

Many passengers worry about matters that the pilot takes for granted, such as how to get in and out of the basket when the pilot just seems to hop in like a monkey. So point out the location of any footholds and demonstrate if necessary. Unless the basket is partitioned tell the passengers where you want them to stand. But most important of all is the need to impress upon the passengers the importance of the landing drill. For passenger-ride balloons the backward-facing posture has become the norm and partitioned baskets make this both comfortable and extremely secure. In smaller unpartitioned baskets it may be appropriate for the passengers to turn sideways, which enables them to watch the progress of the landing, and to hold on to the internal handles, one at the rear and one

at the front of the basket. Posture is to crouch slightly, bending the knees but not squatting down on the heels. Warn of the danger of contact with hard objects in the basket such as the cylinder rims or fire extinguisher.

This posture should be practised once the passengers are on board and prior to the take-off, and a reminder of the landing procedures should be given towards the end of the flight when the pilot still has the opportunity to give it his proper attention. I usually ask passengers to stash away any cameras or loose equipment about five minutes or so before I start the landing approach. This is a busy time for the pilot, but you must visually check that everyone is properly prepared for what is coming up. Occasionally, firmer instructions will have to be given to ensure that passengers are getting ready, and a hand on the shoulder can reinforce the message. I find that it often helps to count down to the moment of impact and I often deliberately count, 'Five, four, three, three and a half . . .' just to ease the tension a little. Passengers must be reminded to stay in the basket after landing until the pilot gives permission to disembark, and on landing a firm instruction of 'Stay in the basket!' leaves no doubt about who is in command.

Most passengers are curious enough about how the balloon functions to ask questions throughout the flight, and this offers the ideal opportunity to run over the basic operation of the burner, controls and fuel shut-off without labouring the point of possible pilot incapacity.

In addition to briefing the passengers before the flight, any of their friends or family who intend to follow the balloon by car also need to be informed about what to expect and what to do. This is covered in Chapter 8 on The Art of Retrieving.

A balloon naturally attracts spectators and the curious like a magnet, and it is important that the pilot also takes their safety into account during the inflation and launch. Onlookers should be politely but firmly moved to a safe distance – at least 60ft (20m), or if in doubt then behind the retrieve vehicle. Take particular care that none of them, especially any over-excited children, gets in the way of the crownline or the restraint line from the burner frame to the vehicle, and in particular keep people away from the fan – potentially one of the most dangerous pieces of ballooning equipment on the launch field. Its whirling blades will make mincemeat of any little fingers poked through the guard, and the fan's powerful suction can all too easily pull in any loose clothing or even long hair.

THE HOT INFLATION

The most magical moment of any balloon flight, this is when the lifeless tent of fabric fills with hot air and comes alive.

After giving the signal to the crownline crew and checking that all bystanders are clear of the balloon, the technique for the pilot is to start with a few short burns aimed into the centre of the rounded envelope, then longer ones tilting the burners upwards as the envelope lifts off the ground. Care must be taken not to burn the fabric, and as the balloon stands up the pilot needs to step back and into the basket in order to stay at the controls.

If for some reason the balloon has risen too quickly and does not contain enough hot air, it will tend to bubble at the top leaving the bottom of the envelope slack. In this situation take your time and only fire the burner when you are sure of not damaging the fabric. The mouth will tend to suck in each time the burner is fired, so be patient and allow the envelope to breathe out again. If necessary it is always better to start the inflation again rather than risk burning the balloon.

PRE TAKE-OFF CHECKS

At last the balloon is upright and the passengers are on board – you've got them into the basket promptly as their weight helps to stabilize the balloon – and they are fully briefed. It is time to go through the final preflight checks, and a PuT will be expected to demonstrate some sort of system for carrying these out. Some pilots use a verbal mnemonic but this has the potential for error and I would recommend a written checklist to be kept either in the pilot's flight bag or perhaps laminated and attached somewhere inside the basket itself – even if it is only to double-check that everything has been covered. Either way it is good practice to start from the top of the balloon and work downwards.

Is the parachute in position, are the control lines attached to the burner frame or basket, operating freely and free of knots? Before flight the parachute needs to be opened to release the Velcro tabs and to check that it is functioning correctly. Note that the chute is rigged to return to position with the Velcros slightly out of line. This is quite deliberate on the part of the manufacturer as the Velcros are only intended to hold the parachute in position during the inflation. (Specific check procedures will vary with different balloons and deflation systems – the manufacturer's manual should be referred to.) Is the temperature flag in place? This is held by a metal solder link that melts at a predetermined temperature to drop the flag into the basket and warn the pilot that the balloon is being overheated.

Check down the envelope for any damage to the load tapes or fabric. The flying wires should not be crossed. Is the scoop or skirt properly attached? The crownline should be attached to the load frame and within easy reach of the pilot. All karabiners are screwed shut. Burners are on and functioning properly. There is sufficient fuel for the intended flight.

Equipment in the basket should include:

- Alternative sources of ignition.
- Maps – local and an up-to-date aeronautical chart.
- Instruments (altimeter is mandatory).
- Radio – check that it works and that the retrieve can hear you.
- Retrieve crew briefed and keys still in the car!
- First-aid kit and fire extinguisher.
- Handling line carried.

THE TAKE-OFF

All preflight checks are completed and now it's time to get airborne. Take a moment to look around – are any bystanders in the way, are you aware of all downwind obstacles? If other balloons are launching in the area is the sky above clear – ask the crew to have a good look.

Using longer blasts of the burner the envelope is heated to obtain the right amount of lift. One way to assess this is to ask the crew to take their weight off the basket rim with a clear instruction of 'Hands off'. If still heavy instruct 'Hands on' and heat some more. On a calm day it is quite feasible to do away without this weighing-off procedure and with experience the pilot will be able to judge the amount of lift attained quite accurately. When everything is ready the people on the ground need to stand clear, the quick-release is pulled and the balloon is free to fly.

Almost buoyant and ready for the off – note the quick-release mechanism going from the rear karabiners.

7 In Flight

There's an old adage in aviation that states: 'The higher you are, the safer you are, and not the other way around'. And there's certainly a degree of truth in this for the balloonist; after all there is precious little to bump into once you get into the air. It is the getting off the ground in the first place, and getting back on to it in one piece, that are the most critical parts of a flight – whether by hot-air balloon or any other type of aircraft.

In the last section we looked at the pre-flight and take-off procedures, and the dangers of downwind obstacles and the risk of false lift. Yet it is surprising how frequently a less experienced pilot seems to forget these hazards once the basket leaves the ground and their concentration is lost in the excitement of the moment and the urge to wave goodbye to one and all. The result is that the balloon will rise a little above tree-top height and will then gracefully fall back to earth before the pilot realizes what is happening and can remedy the situation. So keep concentrating as the balloon leaves the ground and be prepared to put in more heat in good time if necessary.

USING THE BURNERS

Knowing when to burn, and when not to, is all a matter of what you are trying to make the balloon do – whether you are initiating a climb, maintaining level flight or making a descent. Unfortunately there is no magic formula giving a ratio of so many seconds of burning and so many seconds off, because it depends on factors such as the ambient temperature of the day, the pressure of the propane in the flight tanks and how heavily the balloon is loaded.

Added to this collection of variables there is the matter of the balloon's own inertia. The large volume of air contained within the envelope, pushing upwards or downwards against the outside air, creates an inertia of several tons that makes it sluggish in initiating or stopping a movement up or down. Accordingly, acceleration is not rapid and there is always a delayed response time following the use of the burner, something that can only be learnt through hands-on experience. Although a balloon is a simple craft to fly it does require a certain level of concentration at all times. It is not unknown

The moment of lifting off never palls.

for an instructor to distract the PuT in conversation or with a little map reading exercise to test whether they are still aware of the balloon's status. In extreme cases a descending balloon has hit the ground with the pupil still unaware until the actual moment of impact!

In winter the physics favour the performance of the hot-air balloon, as it is the difference between the ambient temperature outside and the envelope's internal temperature that generates the lift. But, in practice, flying a balloon in winter is more demanding, as the burner output is greatly reduced because of lower pressure in the cold fuel cylinders. And even though the load charts indicate that the balloon is capable of carrying a bigger load in winter, it is advisable to fly with a lighter load – at least until more experience has been gained in these conditions.

FUEL MANAGEMENT

Keeping track of the propane consumption and the level of reserves during the flight is very important. But as mentioned in Chapter 9 on propane and fuel cylinders, a difficulty arises because the gauges only give an indication of fuel levels between 35 per cent and 5 per cent full. Therefore the pilot needs to pay particular attention to which flight cylinder is in use at any time and to note its flight duration when it is depleted. Keeping tabs on the cylinders can be a little confusing for the trainee pilot, as a balloon will naturally tend to rotate gradually throughout the flight. Make sure that you always know which is the front and the back of the basket – mark it in some way if necessary – and remember which cylinders are in use or still to be used and in which order. If you haven't kept an eye on the fuel gauge the first sign that a cylinder is running out will be a much reduced and quieter output from the burner.

Most balloons carry three or maybe four

Two tanks with just a single hose to the burner.

flight cylinders supplying one or two burners, and an in-flight changeover of cylinders is going to be inevitable. Before changing cylinders ensure that the balloon is in stable and level flight and well clear of any obstacles. Close the valve on the depleted cylinder, burn out the fuel remaining in the fuel line and when there is no longer any flame from the burner close the blast valve. Disconnect the fuel line from the empty cylinder and connect it to the next cylinder to be used. Open the new cylinder's valve, check visually and listen for any leaks, operate the blast valve and check the burner pressure gauge. If the burner's pilot light is running on a liquid supply this may need to be re-ignited after a cylinder changeover.

LEVEL FLIGHT

Maintaining level flight is an early exercise for every PuT to master. It is a matter of closely observing the behaviour of the balloon and anticipating the need to apply the burners. Whether the balloon is climbing, descending or flying level can be ascertained in several ways. Obviously the instruments will indicate this, but they usually have their own slight response delay and during training it is important not to become fixated

The degree of vertical control is so fine that with care the pilot can skim a basket across the surface of a lake.

landmarks, such as the brows of different rows of hills, an ascent will be indicated when these move further apart and a descent when they come together. You can try an experiment to demonstrate this effect by placing two equally sized books upright on a table. Standing a foot away with your eye at the level of the top of the books move your head upwards slowly and note that the book furthest away seems to rise into view. Lower your head and the edges of the two books will move closer together again. Keep moving your head downwards and the book furthest away disappears behind the nearer one.

It is good practice to use longer and less frequent burns to maintain level flight, both for the comfort of the occupants in the basket and to minimize the noise nuisance for those on the ground. The degree of control over the vertical movement of a hot-air balloon is surprisingly accurate and it is quite possible, using frequent small burns, to skim the top of the trees or to drift across a field within just a few inches of the grass. With time, the need to anticipate burns and their frequency will become almost as unconscious as breathing. It's like driving a car; when you are learning there is so much to consider, but in time you no longer have to think consciously about applying more or less pressure to the accelerator.

In addition to using your eyes to judge the balloon's vertical movement, and to verify its position for navigational purposes, it is also important for pilots to be aware of what else is happening around them – not least to keep a lookout for the proximity and reaction of any livestock. Smoke from chimneys or bonfires can be useful indicators of wind speed and its direction on the ground and this may be helpful in selecting and reaching a landing area. Also, watch for any changes in the clouds that might indicate an imminent change in the weather, or a bank of low-level cloud that sweeps in to catch out the unwary.

with the continual changes on their readouts. Some pilots like to place their ungloved hand just over the rim of the basket to feel for any slight movement of the air against the skin, either on the top of their hand to indicate an ascent or on the bottom for a descent. But perhaps the most important technique is to 'get your eye in' – that is to develop a sense of when a balloon is changing height through the evidence of your own senses. Obviously if you are descending at any speed things on the ground start getting bigger, but there are more subtle clues to be found.

Using the effect of parallax and noting the relative position between two or more

Climbing.

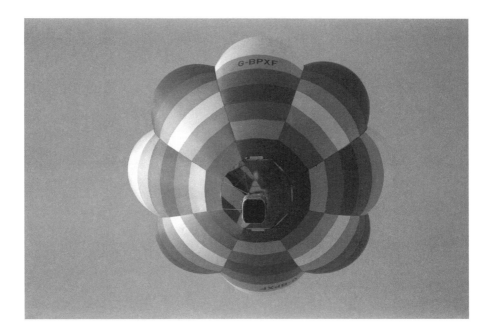

CLIMBING AND DESCENDING

The manufacturer's manual for your balloon will specify a maximum rate of ascent and descent. Although this is usually given as 1,000 feet per minute (fpm) this rate is not usually attained in general flying conditions. It is however, as already shown, important to achieve an adequate rate of ascent during the lift-off and this could be anything in the region of, say, 300fpm or so depending on the circumstances. If the balloon is equipped with a thermistor or temperature gauge this is the best means of avoiding an envelope overheat during ascent.

To stop a climb either stop burning until the balloon has established its own equilibrium, the point where the buoyancy equals the load, or if a more rapid halt is required then the parachute top can be opened briefly to 'vent' some of the hot air. In general flight the use of venting, except during the landing, is avoided as spilt hot air is wasted hot air and fuel consumption will be greatly increased. But in training it is important to practise using the vent and to discover the cooling effect it produces. Some balloons have turning vents and these will also spill a little hot air when opened. As they are smaller than the main parachute they do not spill as much air, but the effect must still be anticipated and acted upon where appropriate.

Surprisingly, getting a balloon to go downwards can often be more difficult than ascending. Left to its own devices a balloon will cool naturally and then begin to descend, gradually increasing to a speed of around 1,500fpm if left alone. That's the theory, but in practice the effects of the temperature lapse rate of the ambient air will reduce this speed to some extent. The rate of descent can be controlled very accurately with intermittent use of the burners to slow it down, or the parachute valve to speed it up. A normal rate of descent is considered to be anything up to 600fpm, although nearer the ground this should be reduced.

In some circumstances it is useful to get

a balloon down from high altitudes very rapidly. But if, for example, you are flying at 8,000ft, even with a relatively good rate of descent of 500fpm it will take you sixteen minutes to reach ground level. That's a lot of time in which the balloon may have made considerable horizontal progress and a chosen landing site left far behind. In training, pilots are encouraged to practise 'cold descents' in which the burner is not used until nearer the ground. During a cold descent the rush of air being pushed aside by the envelope will be felt in the basket, the balloon is likely to rotate or swing and the envelope might distort, although the mouth will stay open. It can be an unnerving experience riding this downward escalator

These cows seem unbothered by the arrival of a balloon, but great care must be taken near livestock.

vertically into the ground but the balloon is still under control and the descent can be rounded out remarkably effectively with a few modest burns. It is a matter of keeping your nerve and keeping your hand off the burner unless it is really needed.

Flying alongside other balloons, especially at some of the crowded balloon meets, requires particular attention. The general rule is that the upper balloon must keep an eye out for and give way to the lower balloon, as the view upwards for any pilot is obscured by his or her own envelope. Avoid excessive rates of climb in congested situations and pay attention to the instruments, as the relative vertical motions of several balloons in flight can easily deceive the eye.

PREPARING TO LAND

Flying below 500ft, or when descending in preparation for a landing, must always be carried out with utmost concentration on the task in hand and with consideration for animals or people on the ground. Attention should be given to the instruments and to the ground itself, while also monitoring your position. It is recommended that the balloon is flown using only the whisper burners to keep any noise nuisance to an absolute minimum.

The choice of a potential landing site will, of course, be dictated by the drift of the balloon itself, as well as the requirements of Air Law – not too near a congested area, inside controlled airspace or too near a motorway for example – and consideration for the landowner. Crop fields and animals are to be avoided and the balloon should not pass low over livestock on the landing approach and obviously it ought not to land among them. And while balloonists might have their own criteria for a good landing site on the basis of ease of access, free of water-logged or muddy areas, and relatively level,

Ballooning can be enjoyed in a crowd, as here at this festival in America, or on your own . . .

*The biggest
annual balloon
festival in the
world,
Alberquerque
in New Mexico
is renowned for
its gathering of
specially-
shaped
balloons
and the
spectacular
nightglows.*

You name it and aerial stunt-flyer Ian Ashpole of Flying Pictures has probably done it – from dangling beneath a bunch of toy balloons, to a high-rise trapeze act or taking a nap in a hammock.

Built by Cameron Balloons, the Golly was the first of the special shapes and is seen here dwarfed by newcomer Rupert Bear. BELOW: *A close-up of the colourful Noah's Ark balloon.*

TOP: *This interior shot of the Ordnance Survey Map reveals some of the internal structure that enables these flying sculptures to maintain their incredible shapes. The map can be seen flying alongside Mr Bibendum at the Bristol Fiesta* ABOVE. *Shown* LEFT *is the ever-popular Thomas the Tank Engine.*

Flying in new countries brings its own rewards and unique logistical problems, as demonstrated during this inaugural trip to Myanmar.

From the snow-covered valley of Chateau d'Oex in the Swiss Alps (LEFT) to the parched deserts of Oman (BELOW), ballooning takes place in almost every part of the world.

In March 1999, Bertrand Piccard and Brian Jones, the crew of the Breitling Orbiter 3, became the first balloonists to successfully circumnavigate the world non-stop – establishing new world records for duration (477.47 hours) and distance flown (25,361 miles).

a little inconvenience has to be accepted sometimes in maintaining good landowner relations. In addition, a landing site should be clear of all obstacles such as overhead power lines or buildings. Even a stack of straw bales can impart a hefty impact if the balloon is coming towards it at any speed. When selecting a possible landing site it is good to have follow-up options in mind should the first choice prove unsuitable or if the surface winds don't quite line up as hoped.

Because a balloon is at the mercy of the wind, not all landing sites will be the most convenient and every seasoned pilot has a host of horror stories about landing in bogs, halfway up the side of mountains or in tiny pocket-handkerchief sized fields. It is all part of the fun of ballooning and it is an irrefutable fact that no matter how tense the final moments become you will always land somewhere, somehow.

There are two approaches to landing; high-level from a height of over 1,000ft with a fast descent or the low-level approach, and the choice is generally dictated by the circumstances on the day. The advantage of the high-level approach is that it enables the pilot to get a good overview of the terrain and the position of any livestock. The balloon descends quickly and is rounded out at ground level. For the pilot the best position is at the front of the basket looking down an invisible thread to the chosen spot. Special attention should be paid to any changes in the lower level wind speed or changes in direction. With practice a pilot should be able to put a balloon down right on the button, even placing it exactly by a track or a particular corner of a field.

The low-level approach is only appropriate in situations where there is clearly not going to be any disturbance to animals. The balloon may pass low over several fields before coming to rest in the chosen field.

Touchdown – a landing in stubble.

THE LANDING

Pre-Landing Checks

- Fuel.
- Parachute-valve line in hand.
- Other lines secure in basket.
- Passengers briefed.

Sometimes described as a controlled accident, every balloon landing looks much worse to an observer than it does to the people in the basket. In practice, landings can vary in nature from a gentle gossamer-like vertical touchdown in calm conditions to the sort of long and dramatic drag in faster winds that will be the topic of conversation for many months to come.

Prior to making the landing approach the passengers will have been briefed (*see* Chapter 6) and any loose equipment will have been made secure or stowed away. The pilot must ensure that every passenger is observing the correct procedures in preparation for the landing. The rip-line to the parachute must be readily to hand, preferably held in one hand, and before touching the ground the pilot lights should be switched off, especially when there might be a risk of starting a stubble fire in dry summer conditions.

After landing, it is crucial that no passenger gets out of the basket until the balloon has been safely deflated. Apart from the risk of injury the loss of their weight could send the balloon off again. Then all flight cylinder valves must be closed off, the fuel lines evacuated and the blast valves closed. In calm conditions care must be taken to ensure that the envelope does not collapse vertically on top of the basket and come to rest on the still-hot burner coils. It used to be common practice to send a blast of unignited liquid propane through the coils to cool them down and to prevent melting of the balloon fabric in the event of contact, but this is no longer recommended as there is always a risk that a residue flame will ignite the propane.

Ironically, the most difficult conditions in which to make a landing are a flat calm. It is no joke to be stuck over a wooded or built-up area going nowhere fast and this is where careful flight planning, given the known weather conditions, and a healthy fuel reserve come into their own. But everybody gets caught out sometimes and the only recourse is the handling line – a long length of tape with a karabiner at one end. Neatly coiled up for storage in the basket, it is attached to the burner frame and the rest is dropped to the waiting hands of the retrieve crew to pull the balloon into a clear area. Of course you have to have found some sort of clearing first as it is no good dropping the line into trees, and care must be taken not to drag it across any power lines. At more or less neutral buoyancy even a big balloon can be pulled by the crew using a handling line.

After landing and deflation the next step is to deal with the landowner, who might already be striding up to the balloon by the time you get out of the basket – *see* Chapter 8. Sometimes the pilot will also need to deal with excited onlookers who want to come to see the balloon at its landing site, and these should be kept away as they can cause damage to crops or worsen matters with an unhappy landowner.

Packing up the balloon is an easy enough task and passengers should be encouraged, although not forced, into helping with this as part of their 'hands on' ballooning experience. Many people expect the envelope to be folded in some precise manner, but in fact the technique is to bundle it back into a long sausage with someone crawling on hands and knees from the basket end to tidy things up and to squeeze the remaining air out towards the open top. With the envelope now in a sausage it is usual to roll up the top fifteen feet or so to keep the parachute and its lines out of harm's way and then, with as many hands on the bag as possible, this end goes in first and the remainder is loosely shoved in in great armfuls until the mouth is reached. All wires and control lines need to be neatly packed to avoid tangling, but take care not to coil the wires too tightly as they could become kinked or damaged.

EMERGENCY PROCEDURES

In ballooning, safety matters must come first, second and third, and as a result we have an excellent safety record. There are three key elements leading to safer flying:

- All equipment is properly maintained.
- Good flying practices are observed.
- Emergency procedures are thoroughly and regularly rehearsed.

We have dealt with the first two items on this list in previous chapters of this book, now it is time to consider what to do if the worst should happen. The type of emergencies a balloonist might encounter fall into five main categories:

- Equipment failures.
- Fuel leaks and/or fires.
- Power line contacts.
- Heavy landings.
- Medical emergencies.

Equipment Failures

There was a time when the procedure for dealing with pilot-light failures was engraved on every balloonist's heart, but the modern burners tend to be so reliable that these are largely a thing of the past. I certainly cannot remember dealing with a single incident of pilot-light failure in my last ten years of flying. Having said that, it is an eventuality that must be prepared for as the consequences could be serious.

The first recourse is to attempt a relight using the burner's in-built piezo striker or alternative sources of ignition. If this fails, and that is highly unlikely, the main burner can become its own pilot light with the following procedure: close the flight cylinder's main liquid supply valve, open the blast valve on the burner and leave it open, open the cylinder's valve just a crack and ignite the resulting small jet of gas at the burner with matches or handheld igniter. It is possible to then operate the main burner by opening up and closing the main cylinder valve only. This procedure is only advisable in a strict emergency as the restricted flow can soon cause freezing of the valves. But as most burners are double units nowadays it is unlikely to be necessary.

It is also possible to use the quiet burner as a pilot light, but again watch out for freezing.

Balloonist Mark Stevens puts a pair of pilot's gloves to the ultimate test.

Fire on the Ground

In ballooning we are dealing with highly flammable propane and the qualities of this gas are covered in depth in Chapter 9. For a fire to take place it requires three elements to be present – the triangle of fuel, oxygen and a source of ignition. A propane fire, either on the ground or in the air, is only going to occur where there is a fuel leak and fortunately these are very rare.

The key to tackling any fire is to remove one of the three elements from the triangle. The emphasis must be on cutting off the supply of fuel as quickly as possible, otherwise if you only extinguish the immediate fire but can't stop the fuel then the danger continues to exist. If a fire on the ground cannot be extinguished within 20–30 seconds evacuate the area to a minimum safe distance of 250ft (75m). Keep all onlookers well away and immediately notify the fire brigade that there is a propane fire in progress and that other cylinders might be involved.

When a flight cylinder is overheated the pressure relief valve (PRV) is designed to open to relieve the excess pressure, sending a jet of liquid propane shooting into the air. Obviously if there is a source of ignition present this will ignite. This may sound drastic, but if the internal pressure were to become too great for the cylinder it would explode with even more devastating results. Once the pressure has reduced the valve may reset only to blow again later if the pressure builds once more.

Should a fire occur when the balloon is already inflated it is important to rip out the parachute valve before evacuating the passengers and ensuring that if at all possible they use their weight to hold the balloon down until everyone is out of the basket.

Fire in the Air

Probably a balloonist's worst nightmare, but thankfully a very rare occurrence. As with a fire on the ground the procedure is to isolate the fuel supply first and then use the fire extinguisher if still necessary. Check for fuel leaks and if there are none relight the burners and land as soon as possible. If the burner cannot be relit the balloon will make a cold descent until it hits the ground. Clearly at around 1,500fpm or 15mph this will be a hard impact, so bones may be broken, but it is probably not life threatening. The rate of descent can be arrested to some extent by jettisoning any heavy items such as fuel cylinders and other equipment if it is practicable and safe to do so. If a cylinder continues to leak it may be jettisoned over open countryside. Advise the retrieve crew of its location and get them to alert the fire brigade. Land immediately.

Power Line Contact

A recent study published by the American Medical Association has confirmed that power line contacts are the major cause of fatalities in ballooning accidents. It is not a surprising conclusion really as power lines are such a common part of the modern landscape, they are sometimes difficult to see, and they carry voltages ranging from 415

volts to 400,000 volts (400kV). In certain circumstances a power line wire can act as a plasma cutter, slicing straight through a basket, its support wires and fuel cylinders. Consequently, the result of a power line contact is likely to be a serious fire with associated injuries, severe damage to the balloon and the risk of injuries from falling.

In the UK the standard height of 400kV and 275kV lines operated by the National Grid Company is 93ft (30m), but some can be 165ft high. This makes them relatively easy to spot and the lines are also marked on the Ordnance Survey Landranger maps used by balloonists. More common are the lower-voltage lines which are operated by the regional electricity companies and these are either supported on wooden telegraph poles or smaller steel towers, and while heights tend to be lower than the National Grid lines some reach up to 150ft (45m) high. The main hazards to balloonists are the 11kV lines because they are lower and often merge into the background. In some cases poles will be situated in trees or hedge-lines and therefore can be extremely difficult to see from the air.

An object contacting a single wire alone will not cause a flow of electricity, which is why birds can perch on a live wire in safety. For the power to flow a complete circuit must be created by either a conductor or by an arc through air which has become ionized. So if you are caught in wires and suspended above the ground, never lower a rope as this may complete a live circuit. Shut the fuel system down immediately. If you are forced to evacuate the basket you should attempt to jump clear, but if possible wait for help to arrive from the power company.

The UK National Grid system has a safety device that is designed to cut off the power supply if a line is disturbed. But this must never be relied upon in the case of a balloon contact as the disturbance may not have been sufficient to activate the system, and

If you contact two lines or more simultaneously there will normally be a short circuit and unless the line trips out you will have a large current flowing that will attempt to burn anything it is in contact with. Arcing through the human body is unlikely unless it is in direct contact with the power line.

All balloonist teams are advised to carry a full list of telephone numbers for the electricity companies and, in the UK, emergency numbers are also displayed at intervals on the poles themselves. The fire brigade should also be notified that propane is involved in the incident.

Heavy Landings
For the most part, the wicker balloon basket is a forgiving and protective cocoon for its

Power lines.

the power will reconnect again automatically to check if the line is clear. On lower-voltage lines this tripping mechanism is less responsive. Do not assume just because a wire is brought down to the ground that it is safe. Resist any temptation to recover an envelope that is draped over or in contact with wires.

Conductivity is not, as many suppose, confined solely to metals and it can occur in most materials given the right circumstances. Arcing through ionized air can occur depending upon the voltage, humidity and the level of airborne particles or pollution. It is worth pointing out that a balloon burner can actually be the cause of ionization, which will substantially aid arcing.

The unexpected conclusion to a long-distance flight; landing in a bog.

occupants. However, there are occasions when a heavy landing is unavoidable. By properly briefing passengers and ensuring that the correct landing positions and procedures are followed the risk of injuries will be minimized.

Medical Emergencies

For pilots on passenger-ride flights it is mandatory to regularly attend a first-aid course and to carry first-aid kits in the balloon. I would like to extend this by recommending that all pilots and crew attend such courses and that adequate kits are carried in the balloon as well as in the retrieve vehicle. I emphasize 'adequate kits' as the standard first-aid kits are fine if dealing with cuts or minor fractures, but seldom have any provision for the treatment of burns. At the very least carry a large bottle of sterile water in the retrieve and a smaller one in the basket.

In addition to the sort of injuries that might be caused by a heavy landing, such as sprains, cuts and bruises, it is best to be prepared for the more general medical emergencies that can occur to anyone at anytime. By their nature accidents usually arrive unannounced and often at the most inconvenient moment, which for the balloonist is likely to mean in the middle of nowhere far from help. Would you know how to deal with someone having a heart attack for example? Get trained, it will bring peace of mind and could save a life.

8 The Art of Retrieving

AERIAL AMBASSADORS

There was a time when a Victorian gentleman aeronaut might have had his balloon inflated for him at the local town gas works, he would then take his suitably attired guests for a flight – no doubt accompanied by a hamper of cold meats and a few bottles of fine wine – and after landing would give the farmer a shilling to pack up the balloon and take it by cart to the local railway station where it would be returned by train. Such days are long gone and probably just as well. The current resurgence of ballooning activity has come about in a very different age and the art of balloon

retrieving, for it is indeed an art, and dealing with the landowners have become vital skills for the modern-day aeronaut and his team.

In some countries, in the UK in particular, the sheer volume of ballooning taking place in some areas has put pressure on the farmers and other landowners. To ensure that there is cooperation and to maintain the goodwill between both parties the BBAC has drawn up a Code of Conduct in conjunction with the National Farmers Union (NFU) and the Country Landowners Association (CLA). In addition there exists a network of local and regional BBAC Landowner Relations Officers who work closely with the NFU

Through bridge-building exercises, such as this campaign to support British agriculture, farmers and balloonists learn to co-exist.

The excitement of the chase – keep your eye on the balloon, on the road and on the map.

representatives and CLA regional secretaries to resolve or prevent problems. As part of its educational programme the BBAC requires all trainee pilots to attend a Land Owner Relations seminar before they are approved for a check-out flight. It is also a good idea for all balloonists to keep abreast of the farming scene in their operational area where there may be particular concentrations of sensitive livestock such as pigs or, increasingly, exotic animals including ostriches. (These have eyes the size of saucers and can be 'spooked' by a balloon miles away. Ostriches are very expensive animals and have a propensity to run in a wild panic until stopped by a fence, often causing a heart attack. Definitely to be given an extra-wide berth.)

The continuous process of education and discussion has shown good results for balloonists flying in a densely populated country, and while the recommendations contained in the Code of Conduct might not be applicable in all situations or all parts of the world, they are still the basis for good

practices for any balloonist. Accordingly it is reproduced in full at the end of this chapter with the permission of the BBAC.

The Retrieve
In many ways this is the sharp end of ballooning. While the pilot is drifting over the countryside enjoying the view, the retrieve crew has to pack away the ground equipment and head off in hot pursuit.

The number of people required in the retrieve team will vary depending on the size of the balloon and possibly where you are flying it. For most retrieves a team of two people allows one to concentrate on the driving while the other map reads and deals with the radio, but it is not uncommon for retrievers to be entirely on their own. In some instances it is even possible to fly a balloon without a retrieve crew at all and I have known of some 'hopper' pilots who have flown for an hour, packed away the gear and dealt with the landing formalities, before hitching a lift back to their car sitting in the launch field. I have personally done

Packing up the envelope.

this with bigger balloons on some foreign trips with great success, but you are relying heavily on the hospitality of the locals and it is not advisable to make this a way of life.

A good crew will have attained certain levels of skill and experience and to further foster good practices in the UK the BBAC has organized a very worthwhile crew training system with its own levels of qualification. But all too often the retrieve crew will be volunteers who have little previous experience of ballooning. If this is the case it is important that they are properly briefed and that they can manage the vehicle involved – whether it is a 4×4 with a trailer, or a van. Throwing someone in at the deep end does not always work. All too often it is human nature for people not to want to look silly by admitting that they do not know how to do something, so the onus is upon the pilot to make sure everyone is happy with what they are being asked to do.

There are a few basic guidelines for the crew and some of these will apply to any friends or family of the passengers who may also wish to follow them. Before launching, the pilot should have given the crew an indication of the anticipated track the balloon will take. As the balloon lifts off and gains height the crew should take a few minutes just to check the balloon's actual track both visually and with a compass. The trick then is to keep slightly behind the balloon but in reasonable proximity in case assistance is needed. Avoid anticipating its course or trying to get ahead as a sudden change in wind direction, caused by localized effects in valleys for example, can sometimes cause abrupt changes in the balloon's track. Because of their size, judging the distance to a balloon can often be misleading and if in doubt don't be afraid to ask a pilot to confirm their position. Keep your options open, by pausing ahead of road junctions if possible, before making a decision on which way to go. All normal driving practices should be observed and it is worth remembering that driving without due care and attention applies to balloon crews too. So avoid reading maps, using the radio or even catching up on breakfast while you are driving.

The crew also has an important role to play in maintaining good landowner and public relations. Be considerate to other road users, do not obstruct any entrances to fields even for a moment, and behave in a professional manner at all times. Once the balloon has landed, the correct landowner-relations process is started and this is discussed below. The retrieve has to ensure that no vehicles enter the landing site until appropriate permissions have been obtained, and try to keep any over-enthusiastic spectators off the land – although this can be almost impossible at times.

Dealing with the Landowner

The next task is to locate the landowner. All too often some well-meaning local will say that they know the farmer and that he's a 'nice man' and it will be all right to go straight in to get the balloon. Maybe they do know him and hopefully their character assessment is right, but the correct procedure must always be followed. For a start they may be mistaken about who owns a particular field and there is nothing worse than having to deal with an upset landowner when you are already on their land packing up.

Locating the landowner is not always an easy task. Sometimes there are obvious clues such as gates and tracks leading in one direction to a particular farm. Otherwise it is a case of asking bystanders or locals if they know whom it might be. Even then the owner might be some distance away and the starting point for contact in this situation might be a phone call, so keep the farm listings from your local telephone directory in the retrieve vehicle.

Who then goes to talk to the farmer will vary. Some pilots insist on always doing it themselves, while many experienced crew members will pride themselves on being capable of carrying out this task. Remember that we are uninvited guests on someone else's property and that correct conduct and courtesy must be observed at all times. Striking a balance between consideration for the landowner and not slipping into a defensive position of subservience is a delicate matter that will come more easily with experience. But a good starting point is how you initiate the contact. Don't go rushing into the farmyard in your expensive and colourful 4×4 if you can walk, and avoid wearing flashy clothing.

Initial contact should be on a one-to-one

basis and always try to ascertain and use the landowner's name. People deserve to be treated with consideration and often this is all that is required to obtain a farmer's good-will. I never hesitate to address a landowner as 'Sir' or 'Madam' – it costs nothing. Exchange contact details so that they know who you are and where they can contact you in case they need to at a later date. The BBAC recommends the use of its own printed Landing Record Cards to ensure this exchange of information.

Take full responsibility for your actions, without accepting liability, and do not offer feeble excuses such as, 'There was nowhere else to land'. It won't wash. Explain why you landed where you did and ascertain whether the landowner has any objection to the crew fetching the balloon. If you have landed in a sensible location, namely on a grass or stubble field with good access, and no damage or inconvenience has been caused, the landowner will usually be fairly happy to give permission. But never assume that this will be granted and be prepared to carry out the equipment piece by piece if that is what is required.

In the vast majority of cases farmers and landowners will respond favourably. However, in some instances the response may be more negative, and it has to be admitted that sometimes a landowner will be angry and upset about this intrusion on to their property. This is where the pilot's or crew's communication and negotiation skills come into their own. Be prepared to take time and to listen. Often an angry farmer is venting steam at the world in general and the arrival of your balloon was simply the last straw. Keep eye contact at all times and listen to their comments. Stick to the facts and try to take the conversation in a constructive direction, gently turning a diatribe into a discussion. If damage has been done then sort it out, either by exchanging insurance information or if it is minor damage

then discuss how to deal with it. Sometimes the problem might have been caused by a previous visitation by another balloonist and you are left to pick up the pieces. Even so, from personal experience I firmly believe that on most occasions even the angriest reception can be sensitively defused and resolved so that matters can be closed with a handshake.

On parting it is customary for the pilot to offer a bottle of wine to a helpful landowner, or perhaps even a balloon ride for themselves or a charity of their choice, as thanks for their hospitality. Each pilot should decide what suits them best and then be consistent. Occasionally a landowner might demand a landing fee and a rate per-person has been agreed between the BBAC, the NFU and the other landowner organizations. It cannot be denied that the increase in commercial ballooning, especially in the passenger pleasure-flight sector, has contributed to this trend. The large number of passengers and the associated entourage of followers can often serve to heighten the sense of an invasion of private land. Having said that, some of the commercial operators are at the forefront of improving relations and many work hard through speaking to local farmer groups or through flying landowners in order to maintain good relations.

For all balloonists it is important to get landowner relations right as you never know when you, or another balloonist for that matter, will end up at that location again. To keep matters in perspective it's not all doom and gloom, and I have met many very friendly and hospitable farmers over the years. There will, however, be the odd occasion when no amount of reasoning will change an entrenched attitude and in these circumstance, or where there is a high risk of upsetting livestock or causing problems, the BBAC has in place a system to disseminate the information to help prevent repeat occurrences.

The BBAC Code of Conduct

Please note that some of the contents of this Code of Conduct may change with the passage of time and all references to monetary amounts have been excluded, as these in particular will become outdated. In this Code the word pilot shall include pilots, owners or operators, and the word farmer shall include farmers, landowners or occupiers. Note that the Code imposes certain procedures on the farmer as well as the balloonist: good relations are a two-way process at the end of the day.

A. For Pilots

Insurance

All balloonists should have insurance cover for third-party damage sustained by farmers. No pilot should be allowed to participate in an organized event without evidence of adequate insurance. Event organizers will check that all pilots have effective cover in Great Britain. All balloons should be inspected by a BBAC Inspector every year or 100 hours.

Flight Planning

1. Do not fly unless you are reasonably certain that your flight path will be over country that is suitable for landing. From May to August pilots should avoid flying over large areas of standing cereal crops in light wind conditions.
2. Pilots should have maps marked with up-to-date sensitive areas covering the planned flight. This information is available in the *Pilots Circular* issued to all pilot members and other members on request. Pilots flying outside their usual area should contact the local Landowner Relations Officer (LRO) before flying. On completion of a flight, please report to the local LRO any information that may be useful for other pilots.
3. Organizers of balloon meets should include a reference to this Code of Conduct in their literature and should explain the main requirements at preflight briefings.

The Take-Off

1. Always obtain permission from the landowner before driving on to a field.
2. Check that during the climb-out immediately downwind of the take-off site, the balloon will not have to fly low over livestock. Remember that animals in adjacent fields can be easily frightened resulting in injury that may or may not be apparent at the time, thereby causing the farmer to suffer loss.
3. Climb to above 500ft as soon as possible to avoid unseen animals downwind.
4. Pilots should brief their crew and any other helpers regarding the position of field gates on landings.

In the Air

1. The Air Navigation Order requires that an aircraft (balloon) must not fly closer than 500ft to any person, vessel, vehicle or structure except where taking off or landing. Use of the quieter liquid fire burner is recommended when coming below 1,000ft to find a suitable place to land. Pilots should try also to avoid flying low over livestock buildings on an approach to their landing spot.
2. If it appears that livestock has been disturbed for any reason, note the location of the incident and check the cause and after effects with the appropriate farmer as soon as possible after landing. If the pilot cannot locate the farmer then approach the local LRO (who will have access to local NFU Group Offices or CLA Regional Offices). If this still proves unsuccessful then seek assistance from the local police station.

The Landing

1. Select a landing field that should cause the least possible inconvenience to the farmer. Particular care should be taken during the spring and summer months when standing crops (including long grass for making hay or silage) cover large areas of the countryside. Remember the risk of fire when landing in dry conditions from July to September and extinguish pilot lights before touchdown.

2. Ensure that the ground below and ahead is clear of livestock, overhead power lines, buildings or other property that could be damaged.
3. If an emergency dictates a choice between landing in a growing crop or disturbing animals, opt if possible for the crops since any damage is likely to be capable of easier assessment.
4. Immediately after landing take all reasonable steps to discourage onlookers from coming on to the field since damage caused by such inquisitive bystanders in trampling crops may be considerable.
5. Pilots should never make tethered flights or reinflate the balloon in the landing field or carry out an intermediate landing unless they have obtained permission to do so from the farmer.

Record and Retrieve
1. Always contact the farmer, or in his absence a responsible agent (for instance close family or an employee), and obtain details from them giving authorization to retrieve the balloon. This should be done before the pilot allows his vehicle to come on to private property. Always use a Landing Record Card approved by the BBAC, NFU/CLA with all the relevant details.
2. Any request made for a retrieval fee should be negotiated along the lines of BBAC, NFU, CLA guidance given from time to time.
3. If the pilot is unable to contact any appropriate person then he should leave his Landing Record Card in a sensible place and take all reasonable measures to obtain the farmer's name, address and telephone number and contact him as soon as possible afterwards.
4. Pilots should ensure that all farm gates are left as they were found.

Post Flight
1. If contacted by a BBAC LRO for further information about a particular flight, then the pilot should cooperate by providing details as soon as possible. If a claim is being made against the pilot's insurance policy then notify insurers immediately. If the claim is likely to be within the pilot's excess on his policy the parties are strongly recommended to attempt to negotiate and settle the matter once the farmer has satisfied the burden of proof showing that the damage sustained is most likely to have been caused by the balloon in flight or on landing.

B. For Farmers
1. It is important that farmers are courteous and cooperate with the pilot. If there is any difficulty encountered then the matter should be handled with tact and the services of the representative organizations should be utilized.
2. Where a Landing Record Card is delivered to a farmer then in return the farmer should agree to provide his own details to identify himself.
3. Whenever there is a difficulty with retrieval of a balloon, then the farmer should give reasonable assistance as requested by the pilot to ensure that it is recovered as soon as possible without damage. Any extra expense that is incurred in helping the balloonist should be reimbursed on a reasonable basis to be fixed at the outset.
4. Farmers are reminded that it is illegal to impound balloons. Any damage caused to the balloon by the farmer is recoverable by the pilot through the County Court. Once the farmer has received sufficient details from the Landing Record Card he should not unreasonably object to the retrieval of the balloon.
5. If any damage has been caused then the farmer and balloonist should attempt to agree a statement of facts as to the alleged damage that has been caused at the scene of the landing. If it is possible, discuss settlement there and then to prevent future delays through correspondence.
6. Failing other local practice any request for a recovery fee (which is accepted without prejudice to any potential claim for damage caused) should be in line with the agreed rate per head.

9 Propane – Fuel to Fly

One of a number of liquid petroleum gasses (LPG), propane is the cornerstone of modern ballooning – the fuel we burn in order to fly, although in some hotter countries only butane or propane/butane mixes are available and these are far from ideal for our needs.

Propane has some interesting characteristics:

- It is highly flammable when mixed with even the smallest quantities of air. A proportion of some 2 per cent to 10 per cent of propane in a propane and air mixture is flammable, and atmospheres containing over 10 per cent of propane can be explosive.
- It is entirely colourless as a gas, although it is visible as a liquid white spray when vented from a fuel cylinder.
- It is odourless in its natural state and for this reason a distinctive odour is added in the processing to aid with the detection of leaks.

A gang of 47kg propane cylinders.

- It is almost one and a half times heavier than air. This means that any free gas will settle in the bottom of the basket, on the ground or collect in containers, hollows or drains.
- Stored as a liquid under low pressure, the gas 'boils off' when this pressure is released. Propane at 20°C is at a pressure of some 100psi. And if released, a given volume of liquid propane will form some 270 volumes of gas.
- When propane is changing from a liquid to a gas there is a sharp drop in temperature, which can cause cold burns on the skin and can also cause water vapour to freeze inside an open valve, blocking it open.

The Anatomy of a Fuel Cylinder

There was a time when most balloonists used only one type of flight cylinder – the trusty Worthington. Produced in the USA for propane-driven forklift trucks, they are constructed of aluminium and hold 40 litres of fuel – so they are not too heavy to carry or to heave in and out of a balloon basket. Nowadays the Worthington has been largely superseded by a whole family of stainless steel cylinders available in a wide range of sizes and, for the ultra weight conscious with money to spare, there are even titanium cylinders – a spin-off from the space programme.

Capacities are measured either in liquid measures of litres (or US gallons in the USA) or by weight in pounds or kilograms. While

Two stainless steel cylinders in different sizes.

the cylinder (almost) and with older Worthingtons it bends to one side of the cylinder – a hangover from its forklift days when it was mounted horizontally. When vertical, this bent dip will draw liquid propane, but care must be taken when the basket is turned on its side for inflation to ensure that the dip is pointing downwards into liquid and not upwards into vapour. Get this horizontal orientation wrong and the inflation is not going to go well. The inevitable consequence of this mistake is a smaller, quieter and weaker vapour flame, but it is amazing how many pilots fail to notice the obvious and push on regardless. In addition the vapour withdrawal causes the cylinder to cool and therefore to remain under-pressurized for the rest of the flight. Fortunately, two circular holes in the protective top rim of the cylinder (intended for their attachment to the forklifts) indicate the downward side when the cylinder is horizontal.

The other vertical pipe in the centre of the cylinder holds a float in place that acts upon a bevel gear turning a central spindle. The movement of this spindle is transmitted to a gauge at the top of the cylinder by magnetic force directly through the aluminium. Because a cylinder is tall and thin the float can only move so far and this means that the fuel gauge only registers the contents from 5 per cent to 30 per cent full, a definite shortcoming that has yet to be solved. Then there's the slightly confusing way that some gauges are laid out, which makes it all to easy to misread 30 per cent or more full as 5 per cent and less. All the more reason to closely monitor fuel consumption in flight and to keep track of which cylinders are being used.

There are three further outlets at the top of the cylinder: vapour, the bleed screw and the pressure relief valve.

While many newer burners use the same liquid supply for both the pilot light and the main burner, and hence only have one hose

propane is usually sold and metered by the litre, it is useful for load calculation purposes to know the weights of the flight cylinders when either empty or full. It is a lucky co-incidence for the purposes of conversion that 1ltr of propane weighs almost exactly 1lb. The Worthington cylinder for example holds 40ltr or 40lb of propane and weighs less than 80lb when full. In general, cylinder sizes have increased over the years and the norm at present seems to be the 45ltr or 60ltr cylinder – even 80ltr monsters for bigger balloons, but the larger sizes are more than one person can comfortably or safely lift on their own.

A closer examination of the Worthington reveals much about how a fuel cylinder functions and explains the importance of following correct procedures.

The main dip tube passes from the liquid take-off valve down to the bottom of

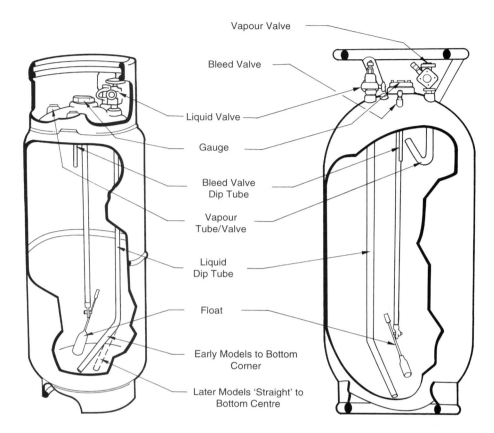

Flight cylinders – aluminium Worthington (left) and typical stainless steel.

The top of a stainless steel cylinder with contents gauge in the centre, PRV on the left, bleed valve top left and main outlet valve top right.

from the cylinder to the burner, some still require a separate vapour supply for the pilot light. Worthingtons equipped with a vapour outlet normally have a silver tap for the liquid valve and a separate red tap for the vapour, and the latter can be used to shut off the pilot light in a hurry. Cylinders without a vapour outlet are known as 'slaves' whereas those with them are known as 'masters'. The liquid valve is operated by a single tap or sometimes a lever. The advantage of a lever is that you can tell at a glance whether it is in the on position upwards, or down for off. It is also a much quicker way to shut off the supply.

Modern cylinders, both stainless steel and

Worthingtons, have what are known as 'straight' dips although in fact they bend slightly to the middle of the cylinder's bottom, and the manufacturers apply labels to ensure that the vapour outlet is on the correct side and pointing into vapour and not liquid during inflation. Regardless of whether a vapour outlet is actually fitted or not most cylinders will have a label indicating the right way up.

The bleed screw valve has a narrow dip tube that extends only partially into the cylinder. This plays a vital role during the refuelling process indicating when the liquid reaches the level of the tube. Refuelling must be stopped at that point to ensure that an adequate expansion space remains at the top of the cylinder.

The final outlet is the pressure relief valve (PRV), which is designed to blow off to vent liquid in order to prevent an explosion should the internal pressure of the cylinder rise too high (*see* 'Emergencies' at the end of this chapter).

In addition to the different types of cylinders there are two main types of connectors in use, the Rego and the Tema, and these are entirely incompatible with each other. The Rego has a screw thread, a male on the cylinders and a female on the hose. The Tema, on the other hand, has a push on action with a lock mechanism – again male on the cylinder and female on the hose. The advantage of the Tema is that it can be quickly released by pulling back the outer collar, whereas the Rego has to be unscrewed. At the end of the day it is a matter of personal choice, although some manufacturers clearly prefer one system to the other.

If you intend travelling abroad with your balloon don't get caught out by fuel connector incompatibility problems – the seasoned balloonist will always carry a set of adaptors to cover all eventualities. While they are acceptable for refuelling purposes adaptors should never be used in flight.

The fuel hoses themselves are reinforced internally with wire braid to give strength and to resist day-to-day damage.

REFUELLING

Refuelling the flight cylinders must be undertaken in a well-ventilated refuelling area, where any vapour or gas can disperse readily – on still days the vapour or gas may remain in the area for some time after re-fuelling has been completed. Grass or earth sites are preferred to hard or gravelled surfaces because of the risk of sparks being created from footwear or metal equipment.

Ensure that the minimum number of crew is in the area and that all other persons are well clear of the potential hazards. Whenever possible it is advisable to refuel with assistance on hand.

Warning signs should be displayed stating 'LPG' and 'No Smoking'. The crew should wear natural-fibre clothing that covers arms and legs, and they must wear stout protective gloves. Some experts also suggest the wearing of protective goggles. Keep all

A Tema female push-on connector beside a Rego male screw-on – total incompatibility.

Obtaining fuel on foreign trips can be difficult – refuelling Madagascan style with gravity assisting the supply from an upturned 47.

matches, mobile phones, radios or other sources of ignition out of the area. That may sound obvious, but I know of one pilot who triggered an explosion after refuelling when he decided to test that the piezo igniter on his burner was working properly!

It is recommended that flight cylinders are always removed from the basket for refuelling in order to prevent any leaked gas from accumulating in the bottom of the basket or trailer. It is also advisable to isolate each cylinder from the others. With bigger balloons, however, this is not always practicable and in these circumstances cylinders must be earthed by attaching a special multi-

clip lead that is connected to a metal spike firmly driven into the ground. Venting tubes long enough to discharge over the basket top and clear of the trailer should be attached to the flight cylinder bleed valves.

Always ensure that a suitable fire extinguisher is to hand *outside of the basket*.

Liquid propane is supplied commercially in two forms. For those with a location meeting the safety requirements of the gas company, and one that is not going to disturb the neighbours after an evening flight, there is the convenience of a bulk-tank – much like the central heating tanks outside some homes – and depending on their size they hold 1,000 or even 2,000ltr. While most of these supply the liquid propane through internal pressure aided by gravity, some are fitted with hand pumps or, luxury of luxuries, a protected electrical pump. For the less fortunate the propane comes in heavy steel cylinders. In the EU these are coloured red and they used to be known in the UK as '104s' ('one-o-fours') as they held 104lb, but are now more commonly known by their capacity in kilograms as '47s'.

When refuelling from 47s the particular type of this cylinder being used must be determined as they are available with a liquid take-off (duo-valve) or a vapour-only take-off valve. The liquid take-off type of

Propane bulk tank.

cylinder can be used upright to supply the flight cylinder, but if the tank has a vapour take-off it must be inverted to obtain liquid. This should be carried out with care and the cylinder firmly secured at an angle of about 45 degrees in order to trap any solid residues or water in the shoulder of the cylinder and to give access to the valve.

Refuelling Flight Cylinders

- Ensure that both supply and flight cylinder valves are closed.
- Connect refuelling hose from the supply cylinder or bulk-tank to the flight cylinder.
- Open the supply cylinder or bulk-tank valve.
- Check for leaks.
- Open the flight cylinder valve.
- Check again for leaks, and check that liquid propane is flowing into the flight cylinder. You might be able to hear it, or even feel the flow by lightly squeezing the hose.
- Open the bleed screw valve on the flight cylinder. (This will hiss loudly while open.)
- Watch the flight cylinder's contents gauge to check the progress of the filling.
- Watch for a squirt of liquid propane from the bleed screw valve, indicating that the flight cylinder is full, and immediately close the flight cylinder valve.
- Close the bleed screw valve.
- Close the supply cylinder or bulk-tank valve.
- Disconnect the flight cylinder from the supply hose.

After refuelling, the supply hose must be vented of all propane before being stored.

Because there is a small distance between the point at which the liquid valve on the flight cylinder operates and the seal at the mouth of its opening, a small amount of propane is trapped in this space during re-fuelling. This must be released by 'popping' the seal using a non-metallic object in order to prevent problems. Wear protective gloves and make absolutely sure the valve is shut before popping or you will release a jet of liquid propane, which can cause severe cold burns when in contact with skin or can damage the eyes.

When attaching fuel hoses ensure that all mating surfaces are undamaged, and clean of dirt or grease. After connecting hoses check for leaks by feel, smell and sound. Confirmation of a suspected leak can be made using soapy water or a proprietary bubble spray. Under no circumstances look for a leak in the dark with a naked flame!

STORAGE AND HANDLING

Propane cylinders should always be stored in a well-ventilated area, and away from drains and hollows in which any escaped propane could collect. They should be stored at least 13ft (4m) from all sources of ignition such as electrical appliances, switchboards and naked flames. They should not be stored with other combustible fuels or exposed to excessive heat. It is recommended that the number of cylinders stored should be kept to a minimum. No more than four flight cylinders should be stored together.

When moving cylinders treat them with respect and, if they are transported in vehicles or trailers, they should be secured to prevent movement and whenever possible in an upright position as there is a risk that the propane sloshing from end to end in a horizontally transported cylinder could snap one of the dip tubes. All vehicles or trailers used to transport LPG cylinders should be equipped with low-level vents to allow the escape of any leakage, preventing a build-up of a potentially explosive mixture.

In most countries there are regulations concerning the number of cylinders that can be carried in a vehicle before it falls within

This cylinder was blown apart when the fuel exploded.

further rules for the transportation of dangerous goods. LPG cylinders may not be taken on some ferries, all aircraft and through certain major tunnels, unless they have been fully purged and certified as such. Being empty is not enough, as the potentially explosive mixture of propane vapour and air contained in an empty cylinder actually makes it more dangerous than a full one.

EMERGENCIES

If a cylinder is found to be leaking and the leak cannot be stopped, the cylinder should be removed to an open area, away from the public and thoroughfares. Warning notices 'Leaking gas – no naked flames or smoking' should be erected and the cylinder supervised until all gas has been vented. The cylinder should then be returned to the supplier or authorized repair station.

The most effective way to tackle a propane fire is to turn off the source of the liquid gas or vapour first. If this is not possible then extinguish it with an appropriate fire extinguisher (either dry powder or Halon), but note that the leak may well still be present and an explosive mixture will begin to form again. If the fire cannot be extinguished within 20–30 seconds evacuate the area to a minimum safe distance of at least 250ft (75m) because the cylinder could explode. Notify the fire brigade, ensuring that they understand that this is a propane fire and whether other cylinders are involved.

Any cylinder involved in a fire must be marked and not used again until it has been returned to the manufacturer or authorized repair agent for inspection.

Fire Extinguishers

There are two main forms of extinguisher recommended for tackling propane fires – the Halon gas extinguisher and the dry powder extinguisher. A few years ago these were easily distinguished in the UK by their colour-coded casings, green for Halon and blue for dry powder, but under an EU ruling all fire extinguishers are now coloured red with their type printed on a label.

Many balloonists prefer the Halon extinguisher as the dry powder ones are extremely messy in operation. However, because of its harmful effect on the ozone layer, Halon is no longer manufactured and only a few sources are still to be found. If dry powder extinguishers are subjected to repeated vibration in transportation it can cause the powder to compact. Every extinguisher should be regularly serviced as recommended by the manufacturers.

An extinguisher is designed to smother a fire by starving it of oxygen. The relatively small size of extinguisher carried in a balloon is only going to last a matter of seconds in operation, typically ten to fifteen seconds, and it is essential to aim at the base of the fire, and once the fire is out to immediately cut off the supply of propane.

10 Putting on a Show

BALLOON MEETS

It is always great fun to fly among other balloons, especially when they are in weird and exotic shapes – who could resist sidling up to a giant Mickey Mouse or a smiling cow 80ft tall? Dozens of balloon 'meets' are organized throughout the world and they are a great way to make new friends, see some familiar faces, catch up on the latest gossip and explore new countries. Many regular events have grown in size over the years and now play host to 100 balloons or more. At Albuquerque in New Mexico, USA – considered by many to be the ballooning capital of the world – numbers regularly exceed a staggering 600 balloons!

It is increasingly common for event organizers to impose their own minimum entry requirements for pilots including a number of hours as P1, thereby excluding the newly qualified. Some will also specify particular levels of insurance cover and most UK meets now require pilots to have attended a BBAC Landowner Relations Course. It is worth noting that many of the bigger meets are consistently oversubscribed and so it is essential to apply in good time. Occasionally the meet organizers will ask for an entry fee, although in return most offer some sort of incentive package including discounted accommodation and propane or perhaps free meals and social activities. It is not unusual for special-shape balloons to get into events for free and occasionally organizers of foreign meets will provide travel subsidies for participants.

Of course, an alternative to the big commercial meets can be found in the many smaller local meets, both commercially and privately organized, which are held throughout the year. As these tend to be more intimate, and certainly less pressurized, many people prefer this style of ballooning and socializing.

Information on balloon meets can be found in the ballooning magazines or journals, or via the multitude of Internet listings. Most events take place during the ballooning 'season' but several exotic locations cater for the winter or overseas

A crowded balloon arena.

Putting on a tethered display for schoolchildren.

flyers. Some of the best ballooning of all can be had in the Alpine winter meets, flying all day in stable conditions among a fairy-tale landscape of snow, mountains, valleys and frozen lakes.

Tethering

The need to 'put on a show' to entertain the public at balloon meets, especially during the day between the morning and evening flying slots, has meant that tethering a balloon has become a more common activity – to the extent that it is now part of the requirements for the PPL(B) and the CPL(B). Unfortunately balloons are designed for free flight and are not intended to be bounced about on the ground at the end of a rope for long periods of time. Tethering

in windy or unstable conditions can generate enormous forces on a balloon in excess of several tonnes, and these increase alarmingly rapidly as the square of the wind speed. (The curved surface of the top of a balloon will generate considerable vertical false lift if it is being held stationary in breezy or gusty conditions.) If the wind speed is doubled, the force generated on the tether lines is quadrupled, and so on. As a result, and through many years of trying different methods, the following tethering guidelines have been devised to minimize the potential risk.

The minimum equipment consists of three tether ropes (to an approved strength of at least 4 tonnes) and two steel cable 'V' bridles fitted with tether rings. These will be used to create a 'Y' formation with one anchor point downwind and two upwind. Anchor points should be a suitably heavy vehicle or substantial tree and the owner's permission must always be obtained for this use. A light vehicle, small tree or man-made railings or bollards of any sort are not considered to be adequate.

The 'V' bridles are connected via their tether rings through two inter-connected karabiners – one on the burner frame and the other on the flying wires. The tether ropes are then attached to the apex of the 'V' bridle and tied off with non-slip bowline knots. The other ends are attached to the anchor points taking care that they will not be chafed by any rough edges. The downwind vehicle is aligned with the wind direction and the two upwind tether points are positioned to form the 'Y' shape, the basket being in the middle. It is sensible to make the two upwind lines of slightly different lengths to prevent a collision should the two vehicles be pulled together for any reason. It is, of course, unacceptable for vehicles to slide or move during a tether and if they do it is a sure sign that tethering should cease.

A nightglow.

The maximum recommended height for a tether is 100ft (30m) to the bottom of the basket and it is important to keep the ropes tight to prevent excessive snatch loads. One way of doing this is to have the single down-wind vehicle manned and for the driver to control the height of the tether through clear signals from the pilot. It should be impossible for a tethered balloon to touch any vehicle or structure. The BBAC suggests that tethering a balloon is only advisable in conditions up to a maximum wind speed of 15kt.

As a safeguard, any tethered balloon should be prepared as for free flight to ensure that should it break free it can be flown as safely as possible. Extreme caution should be exercised at all times in keeping onlookers and crew out of harm's way and it is recommended that spectators are kept at least 200ft (60m) away. A broken restraint can whiplash a rope with the speed of a gunshot and I have seen this do considerable damage to a car. Just think what that would do to a person.

Any tether must meet with the require-ments of Air Law, which imposes restrictions on the height of the tether and its proximity to an aerodrome. Check with the appropriate national aviation authority.

Nightglows

The balloon nightglow, choreographed to music and accompanied by a dazzling fire-works display, seems to have become an integral part of every large balloon event. Just as with tethering, the hot-air balloon was never designed with this in mind, but if carried out with reasonable care the result can be a spectacular crowd pleaser. The main difference from the tether is that the balloon's basket must stay firmly on the ground. For maximum glow effect the whisper or cow burner is used and in general the lighter-coloured balloons glow better than darker ones.

In order for balloons to glow to music the organizer will issue each balloon team with a designated number or letter of the alphabet and a colour code. Arranged in a line or group they can now glow on instruction via the radio to create Mexican waves, alternating balloons or whatever the 'choreographer' can think of: even numbers alternating with odd perhaps, or groups of colours glowing together. The important thing is keep each burst of the burner relatively short and not too frequent or the balloon will become either over buoyant or over heated. There is, of course, a very effective means of spilling unwanted hot air, the parachute valve, and this should be used as often as required.

I once did a nightglow in the middle of the desert and I learnt the hard way that a little ambient light is no bad thing. When no balloons were glowing it was impossible for the pilots to see the exact position of their envelopes. We were literally shooting in the dark, and each burst of the burner left us blinded. So take care and keep looking up.

STUNT FLYING

When the eighteenth century ballooning showmen found that the novelty of a balloon flight was in itself ceasing to draw large crowds they resorted to ever more exotic aerial antics to spice things up. Many took to the skies astride horses or other animals, others rode on trapeze harnesses or parachuted back to earth, and some even sent their wives aloft in the pursuit of novelty. Their modern hot-air counterparts have been no less imaginative in the pursuit of publicity for their clients and perhaps the most famous of these latter-day showman aeronauts is Britain's Ian Ashpole of the Flying Pictures company. Over the years Ian has exited a balloon basket in just about every fashion imaginable including bungee jumping and parachuting, he has ridden underneath a balloon in a 'portaloo' and slung between two balloons in a hammock or walking on a tightrope, and not content with that he has even gone for a flight perched

ABOVE AND RIGHT: Stunt flyer Ian Ashpole sets a new altitude record for bungee jumping from a balloon – and how the shot was obtained by a second camera.

on the balloon's crown. Ian is also an enthusiastic exponent of cluster ballooning – riding in a harness beneath bunches of helium-filled weather balloons. But as they say on all the best television programmes, 'Don't try this at home!'

Parachuting and Hang-Glider Drops

As the very first parachute jump was made from a balloon it is only appropriate that balloons still attract the downwardly mobile. A 'jump rating' to drop parachutists can be granted by the British Parachuting Association provided that they are satisfied with a balloon pilot's level of experience.

Providing the legalities have been properly dealt with, the technique is not especially difficult. The sudden loss of the weight of one or more people will cause the balloon to shoot upwards, therefore the balloon must be in a rapid descent from a sufficient height when the parachutists exit the basket. For the parachutists the experience of jumping into still air is a novel one and many first timers find it a little unnerving.

Dropping a hang-glider is similar in theory but a little more complicated in practice. The hang-glider must be properly suspended with a release mechanism that is simple to operate and reliable – usually in the control of the balloon pilot in communication with the hang-glider pilot. When released at a suitable drop height, the hang-glider will tend to fall vertically in the still air before it can assume its normal flight attitude. The most dangerous part of the flight is the initial balloon launch and the climb to the point where the hang-glider could be released and fly safely. In some ways the legalities are a little more straightforward provided the permission to make the drop has been filed with the CAA.

In the UK no one may jump from an

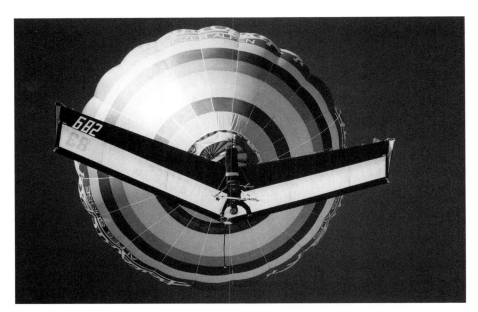

Preparing to drop a hang-glider.

aircraft other than in an emergency without the written permission of the CAA. The aircraft itself must also have the provision to do so written into its Certificate of Airworthiness. Before attempting any of the stunts described in this section it is vital to make absolutely sure that you are complying with all aspects of aviation law.

11 Advanced Ballooning

COMPETITION FLYING

Flying hot-air balloons competitively is exhilarating, challenging and highly addictive. But given that balloons travel entirely at the mercy of the wind, they are perhaps unlikely candidates for competitive air sports. This was the dilemma that faced the emerging aero clubs back in the golden age of gas ballooning in the pre-World War One years. And indeed, as you can't race balloons as such, except by covering long distances, the competitive element is more concerned with accuracy – skilfully using the winds and any changes in wind direction to be found at different heights to complete a given 'task'.

Accordingly, those Edwardian gas balloonists devised several tests of accuracy such as the 'Fox Hunt' in which the fox balloon

was pursued by a pack of hound balloons all attempting to land nearest to the fox's eventual resting place. Many of these tasks have been handed down the years to the hot-air fraternity, which has added its own ingenious tasks to the list. And as if they are not difficult enough in themselves, in order to even out the inevitable influence of luck (not a word to be spoken too loudly in competition circles) and to some extent to insure against bad weather bringing a halt to the proceedings, the modern competition directors fiendishly and almost routinely present the pilots with multiple tasks per flight.

Instead of having to make a landing, competition markers were introduced in the 1970s in the form of streamers usually made of balloon fabric and weighted at one end

Dropping a marker on target.

91

A key grab with the added challenge of a water-borne pole.

with 70 grams of sand – enough to send it downwards but hopefully not enough to damage an unsuspecting cranium. At one time the early UK competitors were required to fit their balloons with officially approved drop-tubes for the release of markers – lengths of plastic drainpipe strapped to the corner of the basket. But these fell into disrepute as gravity drops were not accepted by the international community, so the art of accurately lobbing the marker became part and parcel of a successful delivery to the target, an art in itself as they seldom fall truly vertically. The most skilful drops are made from very low heights and often a bunch of competing balloons is to be found jostling for space over their goal. Ironically, pilots are becoming so accurate in making marker drops that the gravity drop has been reinstated as an optional competition rule.

The targets themselves are either easily recognized landmarks, such as a particular road junction (preferably not a busy one), or are marked by large fabric crosses laid out in a suitable field.

Competition Tasks

Judge Declared Goal (JDG) and Hesitation Waltz
A downwind target is set by the competition director and competitors must drop a marker as near to it as possible. A variation on this is the 'Hesitation Waltz' in which several targets are set and the pilot must choose which one to attack while in flight.

Pilot Declared Goal (PDG)
This time the pilot gets to choose the target within certain specified distance limits from the launch site. The goal must be declared before launching and a pilot will not know which goal his competitors have selected.

Fly-In
One of the most exciting and popular tasks for the spectators. The launch field becomes the target and each pilot must find a launch site a minimum distance away and attempt to fly-in and drop their marker.

Fly-On
Usually combined with another task, the pilot selects a second goal in flight and marks its grid reference on the marker they drop at the first goal.

Elbow
As its name suggests, this is a task requiring the maximum change of direction. The pilot begins by flying for a specified minimum distance and drops a marker before attempting the maximum change in course before dropping the final marker, a minimum distance from the first.

Hare and Hounds
The hare takes off and five to ten minutes later the competition balloons are allowed to launch in order to drop a marker near to the hare's landing spot. Of course the hare will be doing its utmost to shake off its pursuers by changing heights and directions throughout its flight.

Watership Down
Taking its name from Richard Adams's famous story about the rabbits, this is a combination of a 'Fly-In' and a 'Hare and Hounds'. Competitors have to fly-in to the hare's take-off site, timing it so that they arrive, hopefully, just after the moment when the hare pops up and the pursuit begins.

Gordon Bennett Memorial
Not, as you might suspect, a distance race. A target is specified outside of a scoring area and competitors must drop their markers as near to it as possible but only within the scoring area.

Maximum Distance
Competitors fly as far as they can within a scoring area, usually defined by roads, sometimes within a given time period.

Minimum Distance
Fly as short a distance as possible, dropping a marker only after a minimum time period. A target is laid out on the launch field as the goal.

Calculated Rate Approach Task
Goals are set within scoring areas, each having its own period of validity.

Race to the Line
Competitors race to a given line. However, this task is seldom set in competitions nowadays.

Maximum Distance Double Drop
Two markers to be dropped as far apart as possible within a defined scoring area or areas.

Measuring the distance from marker to target at an international ballooning competition.

Despite their heavy workload and the various time limitations imposed upon them, experienced competition pilots frequently score with an unerring degree of accuracy, and sometimes the distances from the markers to the centre of the targets are measured in a few centimetres rather than metres. Clearly while luck may sometimes play its part, competition flying is a very effective way to hone ballooning skills and not for nothing do the same names appear at the top of the competitions honours board time and time again.

Aeronautical competitions, and the setting of records, are governed by national and international bodies. The Fédération Aéronautique Internationale (FAI) was founded in Paris in 1905 to promote the new science and sport of flying and it remains as the international authority that oversees all air sports. Any country may join the FAI and at present approximately eighty-seven national aeronautic organizations or aero clubs are members.

As well as promoting aviation sports in general, the functions of the FAI include defining and verifying international records and laying down rules for international events and competitions. In 1946 the FAI founded the Commission Internationale d'Aérostation (CIA), or Ballooning Commission, specifically to conduct balloon competitions, to promote the development of ballooning equipment and to foster friendship among aeronauts of all nations, and similar bodies exist to administer the other aviation sports. The CIA looks after Section 1 of the Sporting Code, which governs ballooning competitions and records.

It is through the Royal Aero Club of the United Kingdom (RAeC) that the BBAC is a member of the FAI. The BBAC has delegated responsibility for running ballooning competitions to the Competitions Club, which was founded in 1977 and is affiliated to the BBAC. The 'Comps Club', as it is more usually known, has adopted the CIA's Uniform Model Rules (UMR) adapted from competition rules first devised in the UK.

Most ballooning-active countries organize their own national championships and other competitive events during the year. In the UK the Comps Club holds the Grand Prix competition series over three weekends at different locations throughout the country. Performance in the Grand Prix may have a bearing on the selection of the British team in international events such as the European Championships which take place every other year, and the World Championships, held in alternate years. To compete in these a competitor must be nominated by their country via their national aero club.

Any balloon pilot is able to enter the British Grand Prix and it serves as an effective school in which the would-be competitive pilots can develop their flying skills. With the exception of the Ladies World Cup, all ballooning competitions are open to both men and women. Any pilot taking part in a national or international competition, or attempting to break an official record, is required to hold a valid FAI Sporting Licence. In the UK the issue of these has been delegated by the RAeC to the BBAC and their issue to current PPL(B) holders is usually a formality.

No special ballooning equipment is required for competitive flying and a pilot may enter in any type of hot-air balloon. Having said that, most pilots equip themselves with a simple map board and many make extensive use of the GPS, which, at the present time, is not prohibited in competitions, although some people suggest that it ought to be. But there is one other essential ingredient for any successful competition team – a good support crew.

I can't emphasize enough that you don't have to be a pilot to enjoy ballooning and many people taste the excitement of competition flying by acting as crew. They can assist the pilot in many ways, not least by preparing and even inflating the balloon while the pilot devises his or her game plan. They also note exactly where markers have been dropped and even advise on local wind conditions. Some national teams participating in major events have benefited from appointing team directors, whose role is to smooth their way as much as possible and to pool resources and information between team members.

In addition to the crew there are several other non-pilot participants. At the top of the heap is the competition director who manages the event and sets the tasks. Supporting him may be a whole team of officials including debriefers, scorers, jury members, launch masters, safety officers and the observers. Competition observers take great pride in carrying out their duties. Entirely independent, they are appointed to tag along with each balloon team to impartially record the positions, times and distances achieved during tasks and to ensure fair play. It is not unusual for a pilot to invite their observer to fly in the basket in order to more accurately note the exact positions of the marker drops.

The observer system was devised by the British and has been adopted for most international competitions. However, there have been some experiments where observers have been dispensed with in order to save the expense of their travel and accommodation, and opinion on their merit is divided.

In addition to the official competitions, many balloon meets will include an element of competitiveness to spice up the fun flying for participants. These might be just for fun, although in some cases considerable prizes are literally up for grabs. In the 'Key Grab' balloonists must fly to a pole and remove a key, or sometimes an enlarged token key, to win a car or truck. Occasionally the prize on offer has been a complete new balloon! It requires great skill, judgment and more than a little care to avoid ripping the balloon on the pole or hitting the ground in the heat of the moment, but some pilots have almost made a career out of key grabbing.

Long distances

The alternative to a test of accuracy remains the long distance race, epitomized by the great Coupe de Gordon Bennett gas-balloon races which started in 1906 and continued with great success in the inter-war years until the advent of World War Two. In 1979 the Americans revived a similar event and even hijacked the name, and within a few years it had once again become the premier worldwide gas-balloon competition with the winner's country traditionally hosting the next event.

Champion balloonist David Bareford prepares for a long-distance flight with extra fuel cylinders strapped around the basket and, on the right, a seperate Worthington for the inflation.

Hot-air balloons are also capable of covering considerable distances. They have even crossed the Atlantic and Pacific oceans, but distance races are not so common. The one exception is the annual Great British Long Jump. This is held every October and the winner is the balloonist who has covered the longest straight-line distance within the UK. Not an easy task on a long, thin land-mass surrounded by water and peppered with international airports and other no-go areas, but surprisingly long flights have been achieved and distances over 200 miles are not uncommon.

NIGHT FLYING

The great Victorian gas-balloonist Charles Green once described his experiences of flying in darkness as being like 'cleaving our way through an interminable mass of black marble which, solid a few inches before us, seemed to soften as we approached'. Flying through the night, or launching before dawn, can be tremendously exciting and it brings

with it the great reward of flying into the light of a new day.

Although night flying is often a prerequisite of a long-distance or record-breaking flight, for most balloonists it is a case of launching just a few hours before the dawn as their balloons have insufficient duration for longer flights. Timing is important because if you leave it too late, especially in the summer, you won't be flying in darkness at all and in many more northerly locations the summer sky never does go completely dark. It is, of course, essential to plan for a landing in daylight to avoid the dangers of unseen obstacles, especially power lines, and the risk of upsetting livestock. Some experiments have been carried out using powerful halogen spotlights or night-vision equipment to pick out a suitable landing site in the dark, but these have generally proved to be satisfactory only at lower wind speeds.

In the UK there are particular legal requirements concerning night flying. The PPL(B) needs to make two night flights with a suitably rated instructor to be recom-

Swedish balloon-ists launch into darkness to see in the Millennium.

mended for the rating to be added to their licence. Curiously, the CPL(B) comes with a night rating in place, but pilots are strongly advised to get some practice with an experienced night-flyer before they set off on their own for the first time. There are also requirements to prevent the balloon becoming a hazard to other aircraft. It must carry navigation lights in the form of a single, red light, suspended between 5m and 10m beneath the basket, with a strength of at least five candela and showing in all directions. These requirements vary from country to country and in the USA a flashing red light and a steady white light are needed.

The key to successful and safe night flying is in careful preflight planning to ensure that adequate fuel is carried and that the expected track will be clear of obstructions such as unwelcoming airspace or unsuitable geographic features, especially water, at the anticipated time of landing. If controlled airspace does lie in the balloon's path then a phone call before the launch, explaining the reasons for the flight and the particular characteristics of a balloon flight, will sometimes

smooth the way as there is often little air traffic at the time concerned.

Rigging a balloon in the dark can be a surprisingly difficult operation even with the help of car headlights and it's worth allowing extra time and paying careful attention to your checklists to avoid losing or leaving items of equipment behind. In flight it is important to maintain suitable ground clearance, at least 2,000ft above the ground. Navigation is relatively easy in most areas where towns and sometimes major roads are picked out with lights, and on a moonlit night some ground detail is discernible. However, relying solely on the evidence of your eyes can be misleading and the balloon's track should be monitored with a compass and/or GPS and its course recorded on a map at frequent intervals. I remember one account of a night flight by two Swedish balloonists who decided to see in the Millennium in the air. 'We were both charmed by an illuminated red tent on the ground, until we realized it was only our beacon hanging below us.'

Apart from the risk of disorientation, one problem with flying a hot-air balloon at night is the blinding glare of the burner's flame, which causes the pilot to temporarily lose their capacity to see in the dark. So don't forget to take some additional lighting to see the equipment within the basket and to read the instruments and maps.

RECORD BREAKING

One of the greatest challenges to any balloonist is to establish a new national or world record. All aviation world records are regulated by the FAI and the rules are published in the FAI Sporting Code – General Section. In addition there are a number of specialist sections and Section 1, which applies to balloons and airships, is controlled by the CIA. Within the UK record flights are regulated by the BBAC and the rules are published in the BBAC Sporting Handbook.

There are two categories for every record: General, which is open to any aeronaut, and Feminine which isn't – a curious throwback in this emancipated age in a sport in which male and female should be competing on an equal basis. This has been discussed several times by the FAI Ballooning Commission (CIA) but they have decided that there is no case for removing the pleasure and sport that the feminine category allows.

The following records can be set for each of the size categories:

- Altitude.
- Distance.
- Duration.
- Shortest time around the world.
- Speed (for airships only).

Balloon Classifications

Balloon and airship records are divided into several classifications to describe the type of craft – hot-air balloons are given the prefix AX for example, while gas balloons are AA and hot-air airships BX – and their size categories as listed here. (Volumes in cu ft are approximate.)

	cu m	cu ft
AX-1	below 250	(below 8,800)
AX-2	250–400	(8,800–14,100)
AX-3	400–600	(14,100–21,200)
AX-4	600–900	(21,200–31,800)
AX-5	900–1,200	(31,800–42,400)
AX-6	1,200–1,600	(42,400–56,500)
AX-7	1,600–2,200	(56,500–77,700)
AX-8	2,200–3,000	(77,700–105,900)
AX-9	3,000–4,000	(105,900–141,300)
AX-10	4,000–6,000	(141,300–211,900)
AX-11	6,000–9,000	(211,900–317,800)
AX-12	9,000–12,000	(317,800–423,800)
AX-13	12,000–16,000	(423,800–565,000)
AX-14	16,000–22,000	(565,000–776,900)
AX-15	22,000 and above	(776,900 and above)

Observer Rita Boyle examines the barograph trace following Mandy Dickinson's record-breaking flight.

It is vital that the correct procedures are followed for any attempt to be officially recognized. The starting point is to find out what the existing record is in order to improve upon it by the required margin. An official observer must be arranged and a sealed and calibrated barograph will be needed in most cases to provide an accurate record of the flight. Photography may also be used to back up the information before or during the flight itself, although particular processes must be followed. In many instances it will be impossible for the official observer to be present at the landing and so independent witnesses will be interviewed by the observer and their statements will be countersigned by them.

After the flight the observer will unseal the barograph and the trace will be marked with information such as the balloon's registration number, pilot's name, date, make and serial number of the barograph and signature of the observer. They will then prepare a dossier of the relevant information and present it to the BBAC's Record and Awards Committee before approval and homologation. For world records the FAI imposes some time limits: a preliminary notification has to be sent to them within seven days, and the record must be recognized as a national record within ninety days and submitted through the national aero club within 120 days.

The record-breaking scene has been very active in recent years and with so many categories to choose from there are still some great opportunities to push the records even further. In addition to the official records many national ballooning organizations also operate their own schemes, which recognize high levels of ballooning achievement. Highly popular among British balloonists, the BBAC's scheme sets altitude, distance, duration and precision goals with the Diamond award as the ultimate accolade.

BALLOONING ON THE EDGE

When the *Breitling Orbiter 3* balloon, piloted by Bertrand Piccard of Switzerland and Brian Jones of Great Britain, completed its successful non-stop round-the-world flight in March 1999, it was the culmination of a series of spectacular ballooning achievements in the four decades since the modern balloon's revival. Their global conquering balloon was of a type known as a Rozière – named after the first aeronaut of all, Pilâtre de Rozier – which combines the lifting properties of helium gas with the warming influence of hot air as a form of replenishable ballast. The result is a balloon with great duration and, although the first Atlantic crossing back in 1979 was by the American helium balloon *Double Eagle II*, most subsequent Atlantic crossings have been by Rozières and they continue to set many world records.

But the hot-air balloon isn't entirely out of the picture. In 1987 Per Lindstrand and Richard Branson crossed the 'pond' riding in the high-altitude jetstream winds in their massive and aptly named *Virgin Atlantic Flyer*, and four years later they completed the double by crossing the Pacific in another hot-air balloon. Smaller hot-air balloons have flown over mountains, across deserts, at both the North and South Pole, and in every continent of the world. For pilots such as Briton Phil Dunnington the challenge is to fly a balloon in as many new countries as possible and at the last count he had amassed an impressive total of nearly seventy different ones. Each presents its own particular problems to be overcome including obtaining the necessary permissions, finding a suitable fuel supply, getting the balloon and team there in the first place and then retrieving the balloon after the flight. In many cases it is the first time that any hot-air balloon has flown in a particular country.

*Global conquerors
Bertrand Piccard
and Brian Jones
of the* Breitling
Orbitor 3, *which
circumnavigated
the world in March
1999.*

*Travel broadens the mind and often
sets new challenges in retrieving.*

So while the circumnavigation might have been ballooning's Mount Everest, there are many more mountains to climb. The result might not be an official record, as these do not exist for first flights in particular places, although there is still the possibility of recognition by such bodies as the *Guinness Book of Records*. Take for example the case of explorer David Hempleman-Adams. Once described as ballooning's 'Rookie of the year' he made his first attempt to fly with a hot-air balloon over the treacherous Andes Mountains in South America after only five hours as P1, and in 1998 he succeeded on his second attempt. Two years later he made an even more audacious flight, this time with the *Britannic Challenger* Rozière balloon, attempting to emulate the ill-fated polar balloonist Salomon Andrée who in 1897 had vanished on an expedition to the North Pole. David Hempleman-Adams not only flew the balloon to within less than 1 degree of the Pole but after five and a half days in the air he then returned with the winds to land only a few miles from his original launch site on the island of Spitzbergen.

David Hempleman-Adams and the Britannic Challenger *on their way to the North Pole in May 2000.*

Other ballooning projects, maybe even a solo round-the-world flight, are sure to follow in the next few years and ballooning on the edge remains as exciting as ever. No matter what your personal goal there is the great satisfaction of rising to the challenge.

And as for Mount Everest? That was successfully conquered by a pair of hot-air balloons back in 1990.

12 Ground School

People are often surprised when they discover that even a lowly hot-air balloon pilot has to study and pass written exams in Air Law, Navigation, Meteorology, and Human Performance & Limitations, in addition to the Airmanship & Balloon Systems paper. But as we fly in the same sky as other air users and over the same buildings, towns and structures, we have exactly the same responsibilities for our own safety and that of our passengers, other aircraft and the people on the ground.

While this section serves as a basic introduction to some of these subjects – with Balloon Systems already covered by the remainder of this guide – it by no means contains everything you need to know in order to pass your exams. *See* Further Information for recommended further reading.

AIR LAW

In some ways air law ought to be the most straightforward subject as the 'law is the law' and it is a matter of studying it until you know it by heart. Unfortunately it is also quite a big subject including many aspects, such as marshalling signals, which seem totally irrelevant to the needs of balloonists. The air law, or rules of the air, for the United Kingdom are listed in a thick volume known as the Air Navigation Order (ANO), CAA publication CAP 393. These rules have been established to ensure the safe operation of aircraft and this requires that all pilots understand them. They may only be departed from in order to avoid immediate danger. Fortunately for the student it is not a requirement to learn the ANO word for word as many excellent publications provide an adequate précis of its contents. The following information can only serve as an initial introduction to some of the main areas of air law.

Airspace
The lower airspace above the UK is divided into two areas known as Flight Information Regions (FIRs) – the London FIR and Scottish FIR – which extend from the surface to 24,500ft. Within these are two distinct categories of airspace – controlled and uncontrolled airspace. Above this it becomes upper airspace.

Getting to grips with the ground school studies.

The controlled airspace is divided under new International Civil Aviation Organization (ICAO) definitions into four different classifications; A, the highest status, and C, D and E, depending upon whether the flight is conducted under Instrument Flight Rules (IFR) or Visual Flight Rules, and the type of Air Traffic Control (ATC) services available. (F and G cover uncontrolled airspace.)

In classes A, C, D and E, Visual Meteorological Conditions below 3,000ft amsl require that an aircraft is clear of cloud, in sight of the ground, with horizontal visibility of at least 5km. The only difference for classes F and G is that an aircraft flying at 140kt or less must have a horizontal visibility of 1,500m.

Aerodromes
The standard zone of controlled airspace surrounding an aerodrome depends upon its function, whether it is for civil use or military, and many smaller recreational airfields have no zone at all.

For civil aerodromes these are designated as Aerodrome Traffic Zones (ATZs) and are in the form of a cylinder of airspace rising 2,000ft above aerodrome level (aal) and bounded by a circle with a radius of

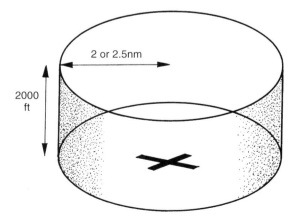

ATZ – Aerodrome Traffic Zone.

2nm where the longest runway is 1,850m or less, and 2.5nm where the longest runway is greater than 1,850m. The centre of this circle is the mid-point of the longest runway.

The military equivalent, the Military Aerodrome Traffic Zone (MATZ – pronounced 'mats') is bigger, extending to 5nm and rising from the surface to 3,000ft. In addition it may have one or two distinctive 'pan handles' extending out beyond the cylinder, in line with the runways and with vertical limits between 1,000 and 3,000ft. In some instances two military aerodromes may be situated so close together that their zones are amalgamated to form a Combined Military Aerodrome Traffic Zone (CMATZ). MATZ are not mandatory airspace but it is always advisable to contact them. There is a mandatory ATZ within each MATZ.

In addition to the ATZ, certain aerodromes, usually the larger ones, will also have further areas of controlled airspace: the Control Zone (CTR) from ground level to a specified height; the Terminal Control Area (TCA or more commonly known as a TMA from the earlier designation Terminal Manoeuvring Area) at the confluence of airspace routes around major aerodromes; and the Control Area (CTA) in which ATC is provided.

Running across the sky like aerial motorways are the Airways, which are Control Areas in the form of corridors usually 5nm wide and with specified lower and upper vertical limits. Their extent is shown on the 'half mill' charts.

One of the worst crimes a balloonist can commit is to enter or 'penetrate' controlled airspace without permission. You are unlikely to get this permission in the busier areas, but many smaller aerodromes try to accommodate our needs and, provided that the correct radio procedures are adhered to, I have always found the military ATC willing

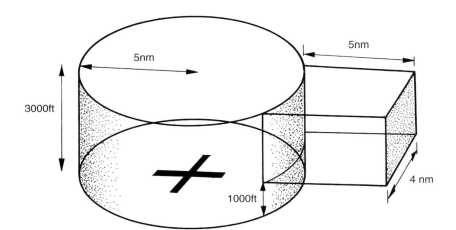

MATZ – Military Aerodrome Traffic Zone.

to be as helpful as circumstances allow. But never, ever, assume that permission will be automatically granted.

Low-Flying Regulations

No aircraft (including balloons) may fly over a congested area – a city, town or settlement – below a height that would allow it to land clear of the area if an engine fails, or less than 1,500ft above the highest fixed object within 600m of the aircraft, whichever is higher. Known colloquially as the 'fifteen-hundred-foot rule' this reference to engine failure, and the notion of gliding clear of a built-up area, seem irrelevant to hot-air balloons. But the law is the law and we must obey it. Only helicopters are excluded from this rule.

No aircraft may fly over or within 1,000m of an open-air gathering of more than 1,000 people without the permission in writing of the CAA and the organizers of the event.

An aircraft must not fly closer than 500ft to any person, vessel, vehicle or structure. Fortunately for balloonists, this 500ft rule does not apply to an aircraft taking off or landing if doing so in accordance with normal aviation practice, but it is still one that should not be abused.

There are a few rules of the air which apply specifically to balloons and or airships:

- A tethered or captive balloon must not be more than 60m above the ground or within 5km of an aerodrome except with the written permission of the CAA.
- For both balloons and airships there are specific requirements concerning the size, style and position of their registration identification markings.
- Night is defined by the ANO as beginning at thirty minutes after sunset and ending thirty minutes before sunrise. Night flying for balloons is discussed in Chapter 11, and in addition there are particular requirements for navigation lights to be displayed by airships.

Finally, to conclude this rudimentary look at air law there is one rule of the air that actually favours balloons. If two aircraft are converging then powered aircraft must give way to airships, gliders and balloons; airships give way to gliders and balloons; and gliders give way to balloons. Along the lines of the 'steam gives way to sail' rule of the sea, they all have to give way to balloons, but don't push your luck on this one.

*Low flying on a
landing approach.*

The low-flying rule.

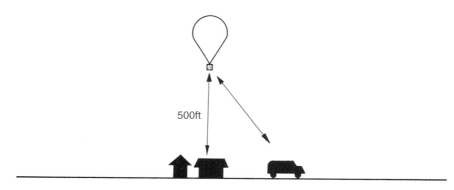

500ft

NAVIGATION

For many people navigation is the most daunting of the exam papers, but it needn't be, as it is basically a matter of studying the maps, knowing your location, and being able to transfer information from one type of map to another.

The surface of the Earth is divided by imaginary lines: latitude and longitude.

Latitudes, running east and west to encircle the globe, are measured in degrees either north or south with the equator at 0 degrees and the poles at 90 degrees. Each degree of latitude is divided into sixty 'minutes' and the distance between these minutes equals 1 nautical mile (nm).

Lines of longitude run north and south to divide the globe like segments of an orange, and are identified as degrees east or west of the 0 degree longitude which passes through Greenwich. Therefore the maximum 180 degrees longitude is on the opposite side of the globe. Note that degrees of longitude do not have a constant width as the lines are

'Half-mill' air chart showing the Humber area.

widest apart at the equator and then converge together towards the poles.

For the purposes of mapping, each country has a system of further subdivision and in the UK we use the National Grid (not to be confused with the power lines) of 1km squares. For balloonists the Ordnance Survey's 1:50,000 scale Landranger series of maps provides comprehensive coverage at an ideal scale with the 1km grid represented by 2cm squares, resulting in just about the right amount of detail and information for the average balloon flight with towns, villages, roads, woodland and major power lines all clearly shown. As the National Grid ignores the curved surface of the Earth, the squares are uniform and, using a simple six-figure grid reference, it is possible to locate any given position to within 100m. For the first three figures, the 'eastings', the first two are obtained by referring to the numbers running left to right on the map, and the third is added by dividing the square into further imaginary tenths. The other three figures, the 'northings' are obtained in the same way by using the numbers running

from the top to the bottom. One easy way to remember which comes first, eastings or northings, is to think of '*Along* the hallway and *up* the stairs'.

The Landranger maps do not show any aeronautical information such as the location of airfields, the extent of their controlled zones and other airspace, air lanes or particular hazards. This information is contained on the ICAO aeronautical charts which cover the whole of the UK in three sheets to a scale of 1:500,000 and consequently they are often referred to as the 'half-million' or even 'half-mill' charts. Because airspace is three dimensional its vertical extent can sometimes be difficult to visualize, so take the time to master reading these charts.

I was once at a foreign balloon meet when one pilot pulled out a chart that was covered in all manner of dotted lines, shaded areas and coded inscriptions. As he studied it intently he rubbed his chin and sighed deeply with the other pilots crowding in, exchanging worried looks, and joining in his woeful chorus. It was only the following day that I

One advantage of an aerial perch is that the maps really do match what's on the ground below.

discovered the source of this 'aeronautical' chart – it was a dressmaking pattern from a shop around the corner! At first sight the real aeronautical charts can seem just as bewildering, but the explanations are all there, contained in the extensive key or 'legend' which identifies the symbols, includes scales for kilometres, nautical miles and statute miles, plus a lot of other useful information.

The complication arises when transferring information from one map to another, as the aeronautical charts work on latitude and longitude while the OS Landrangers are based on the 1km National Grid – although they do also include the lat. and long. references in the margins. Using a GPS or one of the special computer programs can make the translation of coordinates much simpler, and it is possible to purchase specially overprinted OS maps that show the aeronautical information. But the student pilot must still master the art of accurately transferring this information from map to map in order to get through the navigation exam.

To complicate matters further you have to bear in mind that the OS maps give elevations in metres while the aeronautical charts give them in feet. But on balance the navigation exercises are relatively simple: a balloon is considered to be travelling in a straight line and the examinations are based on simple time, speed and distance

A technician inspects an automatic weather station.

calculations. One useful rule of thumb is that 1kt equals a speed of 1nm (or 1 minute of 1 degree of latitude) per hour.

Other distance conversion factors are given under Conversion Factors and these should be memorized. Also, learn the symbols on both types of map by heart, as the legends won't be there on the examination maps – so practise, practise, and then practise a bit more.

METEOROLOGY

The early aeronauts envisaged the upper air as an aerial ocean with its own navigable currents and tributaries, and in many ways

they weren't too far off the mark. Learning to understand these forces of nature is a continual process of gaining from personal experience and building upon a firm foundation of theoretical knowledge. For the balloonist, what is happening with the weather is more of an obsession than just a topic of polite conversation and the novice pilot will learn to look at the weather in an entirely new way. After a while, watching the sky, the clouds, and every little movement of the trees will become compelling.

The Atmosphere

The air that we breathe and fly in is contained within the atmosphere, a thin membrane of gases (78 per cent nitrogen, 21 per cent oxygen and 1 per cent of others) held in place by gravity, sustaining and protecting all life on our planet. The atmosphere is divided into four regions, from the bottom upwards: the Troposphere, Stratosphere, Mesosphere and Thermosphere. But as balloonists we are only really concerned with the lowest one, the Troposphere, which extends to an average height of 36,000ft. Because of the effect of earth's rotation which tends to throw the atmosphere outwards, the troposphere is, in fact, shaped more like a pumpkin than a sphere and is thicker at the equator, extending to 60,000ft, while at the poles it is only 20,000ft deep. Effectively all of our weather occurs within the Troposphere: temperature and air pressure steadily decreasing with height, it contains virtually all of the moisture within the atmosphere. It also experiences large movements of air as warm air rises and cool air sinks.

Only a handful of ballooning's high-achievers have ever pushed up beyond the Troposphere, through the Tropopause, the invisible boundary that separates it from the next layer, and into the Stratosphere where conditions become more consistent. So for the purposes of studying the weather we need only concern ourselves with the Troposphere.

At first sight getting to grips with meteorological theory can be a struggle. It all seems so complicated and yet amorphous at the same time, but there are actually only three main factors that interact to produce all of our weather: *temperature*, *air pressure* and *moisture*.

Temperature

All heat and light on this planet comes directly from the sun in the form of radiated energy. Because the Earth is a sphere, this radiated energy hits the surface at different angles – the equator receiving the effect full on, while towards the polar regions it is at a much more oblique angle, which is why the tropics are hot and the poles are cold. The Earth's axis of rotation is oriented at a slight angle however, so this effect is not constant throughout the year and different parts of the surface become more or less perpendicular to the Sun, which gives us the seasons.

The wavelength of the solar-radiated energy is such that a large percentage penetrates the atmosphere to warm the planet's surface. But this effect is not uniform as different surfaces absorb the energy to differing degrees. Sand, soil and rocks absorb it very readily and quickly warm up, while the sea or dark areas such as forests tend to absorb it much more slowly and take longer to warm, and snow actually reflects the energy. The air that is in contact with the warm ground will itself warm up and rise; a process that is the main cause of weather.

Temperature Lapse Rates

The temperature of the air varies widely, but in broad terms it is assumed to decrease by 2°C with every 1,000ft increase in altitude as far up as the Tropopause. (Within the Stratosphere the temperature will remain

The physics of flying in cold weather favours the hot-air balloon.

constant at –57°C.) This theoretical rule of thumb is part of the definition of the International Standard Atmosphere, the 'ISA' (pronounced 'icer'), but reality is seldom so obligingly uniform. Known as the 'lapse rate', the rate at which the temperature actually decreases with height can vary and this will have a considerable impact on how the atmosphere is behaving and upon the performance of a balloon floating in it.

Warm air rises of course, but as it does so it expands because of the decrease in atmospheric pressure, and when any gas expands it cools. The temperature of a parcel of dry air will drop by 3°C for every 1,000ft – the 'dry adiabatic lapse rate'. But the rate of cooling for a parcel of moist air will be only 1°C per

1,000ft by comparison – the 'wet adiabatic lapse rate'.

If the temperature of the parcel of air is falling more slowly than that of the surrounding air then it remains warmer and it will keep on climbing. It has become a thermal and in this situation the atmosphere is bubbling like boiling water and is said to be 'unstable'. Not so good for ballooning. But if the parcel of air is cooling faster than the surrounding air it will not continue to climb and will sink back. In this situation the lapse rate is less than the adiabatic and the atmosphere is now considered to be 'stable'. Good for ballooning.

Inversions

During a cool night the ground quickly loses its heat and, with no cloud cover to hold it in, the air in contact with the surface will also cool. The result is a layer of cooler air, anything from a few feet to several hundred feet deep, which does not rise and hence is very stable. This can occur in the winter and sometimes even in the height of summer with a high pressure system in place

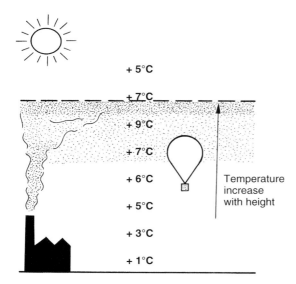

An atmospheric inversion.

resulting in a cloudless night sky. Because this surface layer is not rising it is not mixing with any upper winds and the result can be ideal calm conditions for ballooning. But be warned, on a summer's morning the heat from the rising sun can soon warm things up and conditions can change very quickly from stable to unstable.

In flight, the top of the inversion can often be seen as a clearly marked horizontal line across the sky with haze or pollution trapped beneath it. As the ambient temperature actually increases with height up to this point, any load calculations made on the basis of the ISA will be inaccurate and over heating of the envelope could occur. Far better to take the midday temperature as a safe guide for loading. You are also likely to encounter wind shear from the faster-moving upper air and this can be quite severe on occasions.

Convection and Sea Breeze

Nature abhors a vacuum. When a parcel of warm air rises, other air must take its place. This process is known as convection and on a warm day it will quickly fill a clear blue sky with puffy white fair-weather cumulus clouds – a sure sign that the atmosphere is bubbling away – and as each cloud is perched on the top of a powerful column of rising air they represent a real danger to balloonists. In this situation the surface wind will become quite erratic and a balloon might abruptly climb or descend without any input from the pilot, and the otherwise forward motion will suddenly take a right-angle to the side making a controlled landing much more difficult.

Taken to its extreme, convection will send warm air so high into the atmosphere that the puffy white fair-weather cumulus clouds develop into angry cumulonimbus, the thunderstorm clouds. These almost take on a life of their own and, as they surge ever upwards, they can reach 30,000ft or more

Diagram showing sea-breeze effect.

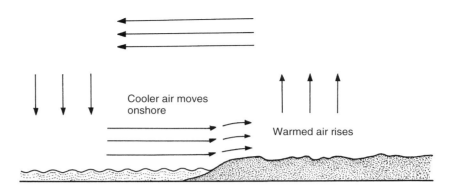

Cooler air moves onshore

Warmed air rises

with the frozen, crystalline cloud tops stretched outwards into pointed 'anvils' by the high-level winds. Within these columns of cloud powerful updraughts would quickly whisk the unsuspecting balloonist to such a height that oxygen starvation and freezing temperatures could be fatal. Even beneath the clouds strong wind shears and turbulent conditions are to be expected. You don't want to mess with cumulonimbus – the only safe option anywhere near one of these brutes is to get back onto the ground as quickly as possible.

In one situation the effects of convection are a little less threatening and can be easily observed. Because water warms more slowly than the ground, the air above it is cooler too and this gives rise to the 'sea breeze'. The warm air over the land rises, the cooler air over the sea rushes in to fill the gap, it then warms and rises in turn and as it rises it expands, cools and comes down over the sea to continue the cycle. The result on a warm summer's day can be an onshore wind of 10kt or more that can reach inland for maybe up to fifty miles. During the night the sea cools more slowly than the land and the cycle is reversed; a 'land breeze' has set in.

How much a sea breeze will interfere with your flying depends upon the difference in temperature between the land and the sea, the local geographical factors such as valleys funnelling the wind, and whether it is adding

to an existing prevailing wind at that time. In some situations it can make inflation very tricky and if in its dying phases it is opposed to the general wind direction you can find that the wind direction is spinning around the compass. The good news is that sea breezes tend to be very shallow and in most situations once the balloon has climbed out of their influence the rest of the flight should be uneventful. Obviously there is a point when the sea breeze diminishes and this usually begins to happen towards sunset when you are looking to land anyway.

There is one other effect of convection to consider. As the sun heats the sloping side of a hill or valley it warms the ground and the surface air will rise up the slope – this is known as 'anabatic' flow. Conversely, on the shadowy side of the hill or valley the reverse is happening and a cooler air flow is moving down the slope – 'katabatic' flow. Although these layers of air movement tend to be shallow, they can be surprisingly strong and a nasty surprise in store for the unwary when attempting to land.

In very hilly or mountainous areas it is not unusual for a cold katabatic airflow to spill down the valleys in the mornings. This is sometimes described as 'drainage' wind and can be in the opposite direction to the actual wind higher up. Aided by gravity it can be fairly significant on an otherwise calm or windless day.

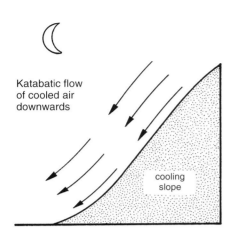
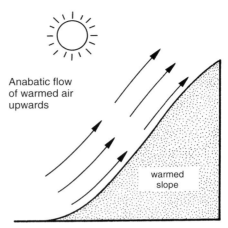

Katabatic flow
of cooled air
downwards

cooling
slope

Anabatic flow
of warmed air
upwards

warmed
slope

*Katabatic and
anabatic airflows.*

Air Pressure

Atmospheric pressure is measured with a barometer and in the UK its value is given as either millibars (mb) or as the equivalent and equal unit of hectopascals (hPa). As with temperature, pressure decreases with altitude at a rate according to the ISA of approximately 1mb per 30ft in the lower levels of the atmosphere. The ISA also specifies a standard mean sea level (msl) pressure of 1013.2mb.

Atmospheric pressure is in a constant state of fluctuation due either to the movement of pressure systems or, to a lesser degree, the heating effects of the sun. All over the world, atmospheric pressure readings are being

*Watching the
weather becomes
every balloonist's
obsession.*

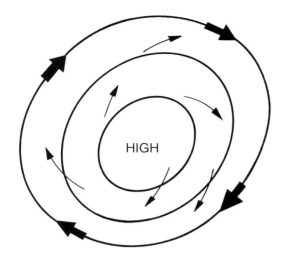 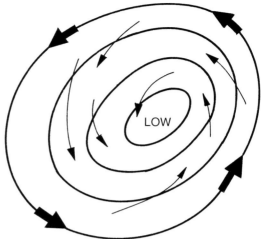

In the northern hemisphere, air flows clockwise around a high-pressure system, anti-clockwise around a low – friction at ground level causes the wind to blow slightly outwards from the high and inwards towards the low.

taken on a continual basis and these are adjusted to give a sea level reading from which the familiar swirling patterns on the weather maps are produced. Points that have the same pressure reading are joined with lines – 'isobars' – which resemble the contour lines on a conventional map. Just as with physical hills and valleys, the isobars reveal high and low areas of pressure and the closer they are together the steeper the pressure gradient, at right angles to the isobars, is said to be.

The effect of these changes of air pressure on the altimeter, and the application of the different settings used to calibrate it, are covered in Chapter 4 under the heading 'instruments'.

Wind

The tendency of air to flow from areas of high pressure to areas of low pressure can be compared to water flowing down a hill, but due to the Coriolis force created by the Earth's rotation the air does not travel in straight lines. In the northern hemisphere

the air movement around an area of high pressure or anticyclonic system is clockwise. Around a low pressure or depression it is anti-clockwise.

There are two forces now acting upon the wind, the steepness or strength of the pressure gradient, which has to be weighed against that of the Coriolis. In the northern hemisphere if these two forces are balanced the result is generally an upper wind or 'pressure gradient' wind, which travels parallel to the isobars. At ground level, however, friction causes the wind to slow down (more so over land and less over water) and it loses some of the force of the Coriolis, causing the wind to back in direction, pointing slightly outwards from the centre of a high pressure area and pointing inwards towards a low. From observation of this characteristic Buys Ballot's Law was formulated, which states that for an observer in the northern hemisphere with their back to the wind the *low* pressure will always be on their *left*.

One very useful result of the Coriolis effect for balloonists is the general rule that the wind goes *'right with height'*. But this is by no means 100 per cent reliable, and of course in the southern hemisphere, as with water swirling down the plug-hole, it is in the reverse direction.

As well as causing friction, the ground tends to present the wind with obstacles such as hills, trees or structures. One effect of large geographical features may be to funnel the wind up a valley or between gaps in the hills, causing the wind speed to increase as the air is compressed. The same will happen over a rounded hillside, the air is compressed and the wind picks up speed over the top.

In wind speeds of 10kt or more the otherwise smooth laminar flow of air is broken up by obstacles, creating a downwind area of swirling turbulence that presents a potential hazard for balloonists. The degree to which this takes place is related to the lapse rate and unstable air becomes turbulent at a much lower wind speed than stable air.

The greater the wind speed the greater the chance of turbulence and the unwary pilot can find themselves dragged downwards by swirls of 'curlover' on the sheltered side of hills, trees or buildings. In certain conditions these curlovers can develop into fully-fledged 'rotors' of air, pockets of vigorous turbulence that can even push a balloon into the ground and may extend for a considerable distance downwind of the obstacle. It is important to be aware of the risk of turbulence in faster wind speeds, to allow enough clearance above obstacles and to note that in general the balloon will be harder to control.

If a balloon encounters an unexpected variation in wind speed or direction in flight, and this is often felt in the basket as a slight breeze on the face or back of the neck, it is the result of wind shear – the point where different air movements meet. In severe cases it can distort the envelope, and in any instance of wind shear the air movement over the large surface area of the envelope is going to cause some degree of cooling. Therefore it should become an instinctive reaction to apply some heat from the burners whenever this occurs.

For information on the measurement of wind speed *see* Chapter 5.

Humidity and Moisture
While the atmosphere may appear to be transparent, the air does in fact hold water dissolved in its gaseous form as vapour. Humidity describes the amount of this moisture and it is the third of the three main factors having an effect upon our weather.

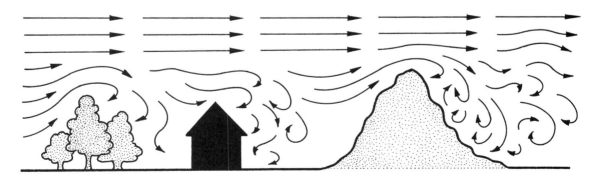

Areas of downwind turbulence.

Cross section of a warm front.

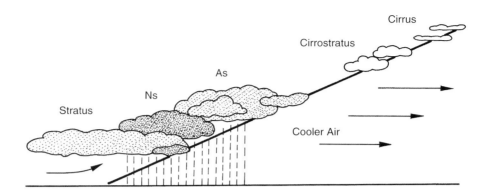

Water exists in the atmosphere in three states – as vapour (gas), water (liquid) and ice (solid). In the vapour state it is invisible, but when the water vapour condenses it can be seen as cloud, rain, dew, mist or fog. In its solid form it is visible as snow, ice, hail or frost and in high-altitude clouds as ice crystals.

The most important factor is not how much water vapour is present in a given parcel of air, but whether that air can support it or not. Air that is fully saturated and can hold no more vapour has reached a 'relative humidity' of 100 per cent. Lesser degrees of humidity are measured as a percentage from 0 per cent to 100 per cent. The amount of water vapour contained by a parcel of air can vary enormously, and warm air has the capacity to hold more moisture than cool air. Therefore, as air cools the amount of water vapour it can support reduces (the relative humidity increases) and there will come a point when it can no longer support it – it has reached a relative humidity of 100 per cent – any further cooling will cause the water vapour to condense into visible droplets. The temperature when this stage is reached is known as the 'dew point'.

This effect can be clearly seen at night when moist air is cooled and the water vapour turns to mist, dew or frost, or during the day when moist warm air rises, cools with height and forms clouds. And if the air is unable to support the water, because the droplets become too big or too heavy, it then falls as precipitation.

Frontal Systems

The characteristics of any air mass – a parcel of air with fairly consistent properties of temperature and humidity – depend upon its recent history or source. Air moving over land masses is described as a 'continental' airflow and will usually be reasonably dry, while that moving over the sea is a 'maritime' airflow and it will have absorbed moisture.

When air masses with different characteristics come into contact with each other things are going to happen, and this line of activity is known as a 'front'.

A Warm Front

When two air masses meet, with the warmer air replacing the cooler, it is a 'warm front' and this boundary is indicated on the weather charts by a line with semicircles pointing in the direction of movement.

A cross-section taken through the front will reveal a long shallow wedge where the warm air rises above the retreating cooler air. This forms the characteristic wispy high-altitude cirrus cloud at its leading

115

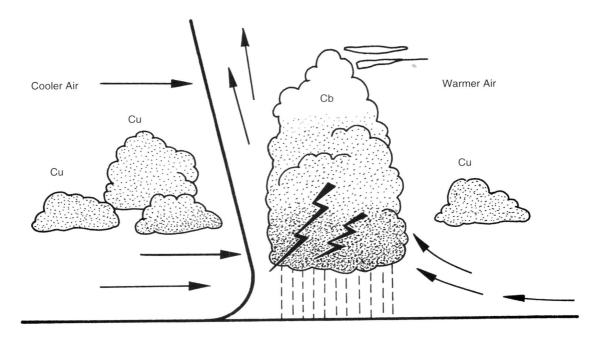

A cold front.

edge that is the first indication of the approaching frontal activity following at anything up to six hundred miles behind. The cloud base will gradually lower and thicken, as the wedge of the front moves overhead and the cirrus is replaced by cirrostratus, altostratus and finally the rain-bearing nimbostratus. As a warm front approaches, atmospheric pressure usually falls and the temperature will rise as the warmer air arrives. In the northern hemisphere the wind will veer as the warm front passes.

A Cold Front

When a cold air mass replaces a cooler one it is a 'cold front'. This time the sloping boundary is much steeper in cross-section with the cold air pushing underneath the warmer air and forcing it upwards. A cold front is shown on the weather charts as a line with triangles or barbs facing the direction of movement. It moves much more rapidly than a warm front and because of its steep angle the frontal weather system may occupy only thirty or forty miles.

The air that is pushed upwards by the front is unstable and cumulus or cumulonimbus clouds are generated resulting in severe weather hazards such as thunderstorm activity, squall lines and severe turbulence. To an observer on the ground the change in the weather is quite pronounced with heavy rain showers rapidly forming, the temperature dropping suddenly and a change in wind direction (veering in the northern hemisphere). Once the front has passed the pressure may rise rapidly.

An Occluded Front

Because a cold front moves faster than a warm front it often catches it up and the

*Typical fair-
weather cumulus.*

result is an 'occluded front' which is shown on the weather maps by a line of alternating semi-circles and triangles on the same line. The effect on the weather depends on several factors, but in short it is usually bad news for balloonists as it will certainly mean rain, unstable conditions and even thunderstorm activity in its early stages.

Ground School

Cloud Types

For identification purposes clouds types can be classified within four main groups:

Cirriform – fibrous
Cumuliform – heaped
Stratiform – layered
Nimbus – rain bearing

They are further divided depending on the height of their bases above mean sea level – high-level above 20,000ft, middle-level and low-level – resulting in the following ten types:

High-level

Cirrus (Ci)	wispy filaments or narrow bands
Cirrocumulus (Cc)	thin sheet or layer
Cirrostratus (Cs)	fibrous layer

Middle-level

| Altocumulus (Ac) | layer of flattened globular elements |
| Altostratus (As) | thin greyish sheet covering the sky |

Low-level

Nimbostratus (Ns)	grey layer covering sky, falling rain or snow
Stratocumulus (Sc)	sheet of rounded masses, light rain/drizzle
Stratus (St)	layer with uniform base, possible drizzle
Cumulus (Cu)	puffy white cauliflower tops
Cumulonimbus (Cb)	towering dense cumulus with attitude, thunderstorms, hail or heavy rain

Visibility

The air in which we fly is seldom crystal clear; one effect of the water vapour in the atmosphere is on visibility. Once again, when a parcel of air reaches saturation point the moisture is manifested as precipitation – rain sleet or snow – or as mist or fog. The difference between mist and fog is only one of degree: mist is said to have become fog when the horizontal visibility falls to less than 1km.

Mist and fog usually develop when a cold surface reduces the temperature of the air to its dew point. Even in good flying weather, morning fog, known as 'radiation fog', can occur when the relative humidity is high, the skies are clear at night and the winds are light, in the range of 2–8kt. (Without a gentle wind stirring the air, the cooling effect of the ground's surface will only produce a dew in summer or frost in winter. Too much breeze and the fog will be dispersed anyway.) Fortunately these summer morning fog layers usually dissipate very rapidly as the warmth of the sun makes itself felt, but in winter the thicker fog layers will actually serve to block out the sun's warmth and may stay in place throughout the day.

'Advection fog' occurs when a warm moist airflow passes over a colder surface that reduces the temperature to the dew point. Coastal sea fog is a typical example of this.

The other form of fog is 'hill fog'. Usually caused by frontal activity, it is in fact no more than very low cloud – although sometimes a rising layer of radiation fog will persist for a little while as hill fog.

There is, however, one other cause of reduced visibility – smoke, dirt or dust particles suspended in the air causing haze. This can be trapped beneath an inversion resulting in the characteristic 'dirty' cut-off line indicating the top of the inversion layer, and it will often linger during a prolonged period of high pressure with dry continental air coming in from the east.

There are countless books on the weather and while the more general ones may offer

A patch of early morning radiation fog.

a useful introduction, the trainee pilot is advised to study those aimed specifically at the requirements of aviators (*see* Further Information).

HUMAN PERFORMANCE & LIMITATIONS

A relatively recent addition to the set of exam subjects, Human Performance & Limitations can be divided into four main areas: Basic aviation physiology and health maintenance; Basic aviation psychology; Stress, fatigue and management; Social psychology.

- **Basic aviation physiology and health maintenance**
  Anatomy and physiology of the eye, ear, circulatory and respiratory systems. Composition of the atmosphere, gas laws and the requirement for oxygen. Effects of ambient pressure. Recognizing and dealing with hypoxia (the lack of sufficient oxygen) and hyperventilation. Entrapped gases and barotrauma.

Motion sickness. The risks associated with diving and then flying. Noise and age-induced hearing loss. Visual defects and their correction. Arterial disease and coronary risk, ECG (electrocardiogram), blood pressure, strokes. Diet and exercise. Fits, faints and the EEG (electroencephalogram). Psychiatric disorders, drug and alcohol abuse.

- **Basic aviation psychology**
  Human information processing, sensation, attention, memory, decision making and the creation of mental models. Limitations of central decision channel and mental workload. Attention in selecting information sources, attention-getting stimuli. Effects of experience and expectation on perception. Erroneous mental models. Use of visual clues on landing. Eye movements, visual search techniques, risk of mid-air collisions. Skill, rule and knowledge-based behaviour. Skill acquisition, conscious and automatic behaviour, error of skill. Maintaining mental models, situational awareness, confirmation bias.

- **Stress, fatigue and management**
  Definitions, concepts and models of stress. Arousal, over- and under-arousal. Environmental stresses and their effects. Domestic stress, relationships, bereavements, financial and time commitments. Work stress and relationships with colleagues. Effects of stress upon attention, motivation and performance. Life stress and health. Defence mechanisms, identifying stress and its management. Work-induced fatigue. Shift work. Sleep management and hygiene.
- **Social psychology**
  Individual differences, intelligence and personality. Personality traits: extroversion, anxiety, warmth and sociability, impulsiveness, dominance, stability and boldness. Types of behaviour. Personality related problems in flying, especially risk taking. Communication, verbal and non-verbal. Interacting with crew, ATC, ground personnel and passengers. Making decisions and assessing risk.

It sounds like a lot and it is way beyond of the scope of this book to attempt to cover such a broad subject, but once you get past the medical jargon it is mostly good common sense, and it might even save your life some day. There are some excellent books on Human Performance & Limitations and a study of these will provide the required level of working knowledge (*see* Further Information).

Ballooning offers a new perspective on our world.

So you have reached the end of this guide, and maybe you have followed up your studies through further reading, completed your flight training, passed your exams, and have successfully undertaken both your check-out and solo flights. That coveted licence is now yours. Congratulations!

But now it is time to really begin the process of learning about ballooning. Just remember that there are old pilots and there are bold pilots, but there are no old bold pilots. I will leave you with the parting words of an old balloonist friend of mine, 'Take reasonable care.'

Glossary of Abbreviations

aal	above aerodrome level		IFR	Instrument Flight Rules
agl	above ground level		ISA	International Standard Atmosphere
AME	Authorized Medical Examiner		JDG	Judge Declared Goal
amsl	above mean sea level		kt	knots – a speed of 1nm per hour
ANO	Air Navigation Order		LCD	Liquid Crystal Display
ATC	Air Traffic Control		LPG	Liquid Petroleum Gasses
ATZ	Aerodrome Traffic Zone		MATZ	Military Aerodrome Traffic Zone
BTU	heat required to heat 1lb of water by 1°F		mb	millibars (equivalent of hectopascals, hPa)
CAA	Civil Aviation Authority		nm	nautical mile
CAP	Civil Aviation Publication		Ns	nimbostratus cloud
Cb	cumulonimbus cloud		oktas	measure of cloud cover
CIA	Commission Internationale d'Aérostation		PDG	Pilot Declared Goal
CofA	Certificate of Airworthiness		PPL(B)	Private Pilots Licence (Balloons)
CPL(B)	Commercial Pilots Licence (Balloons)		PRV	Pressure Relief Valve
CTA	Control Area		psi	pounds per square inch
CTR	Control Zone		PuT	Pilot under Training
Cu	cumulus cloud		QFE	pressure setting for altimeter indicating height
cu ft	cubic feet		QNH	pressure setting for altimeter indicating altitude
cu m	cubic metres		RAeC	Royal Aero Club of the United Kingdom
ECG	Electrocardiogram		RT	Radiotelephony
EEG	Electroencephalogram		Sc	stratocumulus cloud
FAI	Fédération Aéronautique Internationale		St	stratus cloud
FIR	Flight Information Region		TCA	Terminal Control Area
FL	Flight Level		UMR	Uniform Model Rules
fpm	feet per minute		UTC	also known as Zulu – the same as Greenwich Mean Time
GMT	Greenwich Mean Time		VFR	Visual Flight Rules
GPS	Global Positioning System			
hp	horsepower			
hPa	hectopascals			
ICAO	International Civil Aviation Organization			

Conversion Factors

1 nautical mile (nm) = 1.152 statute miles
1 statute mile   = 1.609 kilometres
1km   = 0.621 miles

miles to km   multipy by 1.609
miles to nm   multiply by 1.152
km to miles   multiply by 0.621
km to nm   multiply by 0.54
nm to miles   multiply by 0.868
nm to km   multiply by 1.852

1ft   =   0.305m
1m   =   3.281ft
1,000ft   =   304.8m
1,000m   =   3,281ft

ft to m multiply by 0.305
m to ft multiply by 3.281

1cu ft   =   0.028cu m
1cu m   =   35.315cu ft

cu ft to cu m multiply by 0.028
cu m to cu ft multiply by 35.315

1lb   =   0.454kg
1kg   =   2.205lb

lb to kg multiply by 0.454
kg to lb multiply by 2.205

Further Information

Recommended Reading

Publications
BBAC publications:
Pilot Training Manual
Pilot Training Log Book
Sporting Handbook
The BBAC also publishes the *Aerostat* journal and *Pilots Circular* newsletter.

CAA publications:
CAP 53 – *The Private Pilots Licence*
CAP 393 – *Air Navigation: The Order and Regulations*
CAP 413 – *Radiotelephony Manual*

BFA publications:
The BFA publishes a range of manuals, as well as the *Ballooning* journal and *Skylines* newsletter.

Books
Campbell, R.D. and Bagshaw, M., *Human Performance and Limitations in Aviation* (Blackwell Science) ISBN 0 632 04986 3

Smith, Anthony and Wagner, Mark, *Ballooning* (Patrick Stephens Limited) ISBN 1 85260 568 5

Thom, Trevor, *The Air Pilot's Manual* (Airlife Publishing)
2. *Air Law & Meteorology* ISBN 1 85310 926 6
6. *Human Factors* ISBN 1 85310 930 4
7. *Radiotelephony* ISBN 1 85310 931 2

Wickson, Mike, *Meteorology for Pilots* (Airlife Publishing) ISBN 1 85310 943 6

The Essential Towing Handbook (The Stationery Office) ISBN 0 11 552022 8

First Aid Manual (Dorling Kindersley) ISBN 0 7513 0399 2

Organizations

Balloon Federation of America
PO Box 400
Indianola
IA 50125
USA

Tel: (0) 515 961 8809
Fax: (0) 515 961 3537
www.bfa.net

British Association of Balloon Operators
www.babo.org.uk

British Balloon & Airship Club
www.bbac.org
info@bbac.org

Civil Aviation Authority
Safety Regulation Group
Aviation House
Gatwick Airport South
West Sussex RH6 0YR
UK

Tel: (0) 1293 567171
Fax: (0) 1293 573999
www.srg.caa.co.uk

Fédération Aéronautique Internationale
www.fai.org

FAI Ballooning Commision – CIA
www.fai.org/ballooning

Federal Aviation Authority (USA)
www.faa.gov

French ballooning association:
L'Aérostation à la Française
aerostation.free.fr

German ballooning association:
DFSV – Deutscher Freiballonsport-Verband
Postfach 1333
82142 Planegg bei Munchen
Germany

Tel: (0) 89 89949192
Fax: (0) 89 899 49193
www.dfsv.de

Other ballooning links:
www.euronet.nl/users/jdewild

MANUFACTURERS

Cameron Balloons
St Johns Street
Bedminster BS3 4NH
UK

Tel: (0) 117 9637216
Fax: (0) 117 9661168
www.cameronballoons.co.uk
sales@cameronballoons.co.uk

Lindstrand Balloons
Maesbury Road
Oswestry
Shropshire SY10 8ZZ
UK

Tel: (0) 1691 671717
Fax: (0) 1691 671122
www.lindstrand.co.uk

Thunder & Colt
St Johns Street
Bedminster
Bristol BS3 4NH
UK

Tel: (0) 117 9532772
Fax: (0) 117 9663638
www.thunderandcolt.co.uk
sales@thunderandcolt.co.uk

UltraMagic
Aerdrom Gral
Vives
AP (PO Box) 171
08700 1 Gualada
Barcelona
Spain

www.ultramagic.com

MET INFORMATION (UK)

Met Office
Helpline: 0845 300 0300
www.metoffice.com

Weather Consultancy Services (WCS)
Helpline: 08700 738 100
www.weatherweb.net

Wendy Windblows
Helpline: (0) 114 287 8936
www.wendywindblows.com

Weathercall (TIS Ltd)
Helpline: 0870 600 4242
www.weathercall.co.uk

Index

aerodromes 103–4
air law 102–4
AIRMET 42–3
airspace 102–4
AME 20

BBAC 14, 17–19, 71–2, 75–7, 85, 87, 94–5, 98–9
briefing crew and passengers 54–8
burner test 52–3

CAA 17, 19–20, 89–90, 102, 104
climbing and descending 63–4
cloudhoppers 23, 32–3
Code of Conduct 71–7
competition flying 91–6
controls 28–9
costs 16

emergencies
    equipment failures 67
    fire in the air 68
    fire on the ground 67–8
    fuel leaks 84
    heavy landings 69–70
    medical emergencies 70
    power line contacts 68–9
examinations 18–19, 102–20

false lift 50–1
fire extinguishers 41, 53, 59, 84
first aid kits 41, 59, 70
flight bags 40–1
fuel management 61

gas balloons 22

handling lines 59, 66

hot-air balloons
    baskets 30–5
    burners 29–30, 52–3, 58–9, 60–1
    envelopes 23–9, 53–6
    flight cylinders 23, 29, 51–3, 61, 67–8, 78–84
    parts of the balloon 23–5
    sizes 23, 98
human performance 102, 119–20

inflations 51–9
inflation fans 36–7, 55–6, 58
instruments
    altimeters 37–8, 45, 59
    compasses 39
    GPS 39–40, 95
    thermistors 38–9
    variometers 38
    watches 39

karabiners 53–4

landing 63–6, 69
landowner relations 18, 71–7, 85
launch sites 49–51
level flight 61–2
licence requirements 17–20, 86
load calculations 46–8
long distance flying 95–6
low flying regulations 104–5

maintenance and repairs 32–5
maps 59, 105–8
medicals 18–20
meteorology
    atmosphere 108–9
    air pressure 43, 45–6, 112–13
    cloud 43, 45, 114–18

forecasts 42–6
frontal systems 115–18
humidity and moisture 114–15
inversions 110–11
ISA 109, 112
lapse rates 109–10
temperature 109
visibility 118–19
winds 42–5, 113–14

navigation 102, 105–8
night flying 96–8
nightglows 87–8

observers 95, 98–9

parachute and hang-glider drops 88–90
parachute valve 23–4, 27–9, 54–5
propane 29, 51–3, 67, 78–84
PRVs 67, 80–1

quick releases 54, 59
radios 40, 59
record braking 98–101
refuelling 81–3
retrieving 71–7
Rozière balloons 99–101

sea breezes 110–11
sponsorship 15
stunt flying 88–90
syndicates 15–16

take-off checks 58–9
tethering 86–7
trailers 15–16, 73

UTC 43

winter flying 61, 109